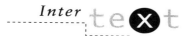

Language and Region

The INTERTEXT series has been specifically designed to meet the needs of contemporary English Language Studies. *Working with Texts: A core introduction to language analysis* (second edition, 2001) is the foundation text, which is complemented by a range of 'satellite' titles. These provide students with hands-on practical experience of textual analysis through special topics, and can be used individually or in conjunction with *Working with Texts*.

Language and Region:

◎ provides an accessible guide to regional variation in English

◎ covers topical issues including loss of regional diversity and attitudes to regional accents and dialects

◎ examines the use of dialect in media, advertising and the tourist industry

◎ outlines the main linguistic characteristics of regional accents and dialects in terms of regional pronunciation, vocabulary and grammar

◎ is accompanied by a supporting website

Joan C. Beal is Professor of English Language and Director of the National Centre for English Cultural Tradition at the University of Sheffield. Her research interests are in dialectology and the recent history of English.

The Intertext series

The Routledge INTERTEXT series aims to develop readers' understanding of how texts work. It does this by showing some of the designs and patterns in the language from which they are made, by placing texts within the contexts in which they occur, and by exploring relationships between them.

The series consists of a foundation text, *Working with Texts: A core introduction to language analysis*, which looks at language aspects essential for the analysis of texts, and a range of satellite texts. These apply aspects of language to a particular topic area in more detail. They complement the core text and can also be used alone, providing the user has the foundation skills furnished by the core text.

Benefits of using this series:

◎　**Multi-disciplinary** – provides a foundation for the analysis of texts, supporting students who want to achieve a detailed focus on language.

◎　**Accessible** – no previous knowledge of language analysis is assumed, just an interest in language use.

◎　**Student-friendly** – contains activities relating to texts studied, commentaries after activities, highlighted key terms, suggestions for further reading and an index of terms.

◎　**Interactive** – offers a range of task-based activities for both class use and self-study.

◎　**Tried and tested** – written by a team of respected teachers and practitioners whose ideas and activities have been trialled independently.

The series editors:

Adrian Beard was until recently Head of English at Gosforth High School, and now works at the University of Newcastle upon Tyne. He is a Chief Examiner for AS and A Level English Literature. He has written and lectured extensively on the subjects of literature and language. His publications include *Texts and Contexts* (Routledge).

Angela Goddard is Head of Programme for Language and Human Communication at the University College of York St John, and is Chair of Examiners for A Level English Language. Her publications include *Researching Language* (second edition, Heinemann, 2000).

Core textbook:

Working with Texts: A core introduction to language analysis
(second edition, 2001)
Ronald Carter, Angela Goddard, Danuta Reah, Keith Sanger and
Maggie Bowring

Satellite titles:

The Language of Advertising: Written texts
(second edition, 2002)
Angela Goddard

Language Change
Adrian Beard

The Language of Children
Julia Gillen

The Language of Comics
Mario Saraceni

The Language of Conversation
Francesca Pridham

The Language of Drama
Keith Sanger

The Language of Fiction
Keith Sanger

Language and Gender
Angela Goddard and Lindsey Meân
Patterson

The Language of Humour
Alison Ross

*The Language of ICT: Information and
communication technology*
Tim Shortis

The Language of Magazines
Linda McLoughlin

The Language of Newspapers
(second edition, 2002)
Danuta Reah

The Language of Poetry
John McRae

The Language of Politics
Adrian Beard

*The Language of Speech and
Writing*
Sandra Cornbleet and
Ronald Carter

The Language of Sport
Adrian Beard

The Language of Television
Jill Marshall and Angela Werndly

The Language of Websites
Mark Boardman

The Language of Work
Almut Koester

Language
and Region

 Joan C. Beal

R Routledge
Taylor & Francis Group

LONDON AND NEW YORK

First published 2006
by Routledge
2 Park Square, Milton Park, Abingdon, Oxon OX14 4RN

Simultaneously published in the USA and Canada
by Routledge
270 Madison Ave, New York, NY 10016

Routledge is an imprint of the Taylor & Francis Group

© 2006 Joan C. Beal

Typeset in Stone Sans/Stone Serif by
Florence Production Ltd, Stoodleigh, Devon
Printed and bound in Great Britain by
TJ International Ltd, Padstow, Cornwall

British Library Cataloguing in Publication Data
A catalogue record for this book is available from the British Library

Library of Congress Cataloging in Publication Data
A catalog record for this book has been requested

ISBN10: 0–415–36600–3 (hbk)
ISBN10: 0–415–36601–1 (pbk)

ISBN13: 9–78–0–415–36600–7 (hbk)
ISBN13: 9–78–0–415–36601–4 (pbk)

contents

acknowledgements

I would like to thank Adrian Beard and Angela Goddard for their helpful comments on drafts of this book. Thanks also to my daughter, Alice Beal, for reading drafts and providing a student's perspective.

ABC reproduced with permission of Sue Clifford and Common Ground from their 'England in Particular' website www.england-inparticular.info.

Map of English regions reproduced with permission of Peter Davidson.

Extract from *Trainspotting* reproduced with permission of Random House. Copyright © Irvine Welsh 1993.

'English Heretic' reproduced with permission of the author and Patten Press. Copyright © Alan M. Kent 2002.

Lourdes Burbano-Elizondo for permission to reproduce Texts 7 and 10.

Clive Upton, University of Leeds, for permission to reproduce Text 8A.

Region, nation, locale

This book is an introduction to the study of regional variation in English, but, before we can begin to address questions of language and **dialect**, we need to consider what we mean by 'region' and, indeed, whether regional differences are still important in an age of globalisation. The *Oxford English Dictionary* (*OED*) has among its definitions of the word *region* the following:

> A relatively large subdivision of a country for economic, administrative, or cultural purposes that freq. implies an alternative system to centralized organization; *spec.* one of the nine local government areas into which the mainland of Scotland has been divided since 1975, when the former system of counties was abolished. *Standard* (*administrative*) *region*: one of the eight (formerly nine) areas into which England is divided for industrial planning, demographic surveying, etc.
>
> (www.oed.com)

By this definition, the regions of England or Scotland are units that are smaller than the nation as a whole, but are seen as both coherent enough within themselves and distinct enough from each other to be treated as separate entities. The webpage of the Office of the Deputy Prime Minister introduces the UK government's policy for 'creating sustainable communities' in England, as follows:

Figure 1 The English regions. www.padav.demon.co.uk/englishregion.htm

There is great diversity to be found amongst England's regions and communities; each part of the country has different economic, social and environmental conditions. This diversity demands a broad range of responses, which form the basis of Government policy for the English regions.

(www.odpm.gov.uk/stellent/groups/odpm_regions/documents/
sectionhomepage/odpm_regions_page.hcsp)

Figure 1 shows the nine regions into which England has been divided for administrative purposes: the North East, the North West, Yorkshire and the Humber, the East Midlands, the West Midlands, the East of England, London, the South East and the South West. Whether the people who live in these regions share the view that they have more in common with people within their region than those outside it is a moot point. The government's proposal for devolution of a range of powers to regional assemblies was dealt a fatal blow in November 2004, when voters in the region thought to have the strongest sense of coherence and 'identity', the North East, rejected it in a referendum. While, as we shall see, people in the North East of England certainly do view themselves as different to those in other parts of the country, especially London and the South East, local identities and rivalries within this region played a large part in the rejection of the regional assembly. The proposed site of the assembly was a bone of contention: Newcastle, as the largest city in the region, would seem the obvious choice, but, such is the rivalry between the citizens of Newcastle, those of the region's other major city, Sunderland, and those of its major towns, Middlesbrough and Darlington, that the historic cathedral city of Durham was chosen instead. A similar compromise had to be offered in the North West, a region stretching from Crewe in Cheshire to Carlisle on the Scottish border, but having the majority of its population in a belt from West to East, stretching from Liverpool to Manchester. If the proposed assembly had been sited in either of these proud cities, there would have been protests from citizens of the other, so Warrington, situated exactly half way between the two, was to be the compromise choice. Such solutions are not unusual: the capital of Australia, Canberra, was created in order to avoid offence to either of the obvious contenders for that role, Sydney and Melbourne.

What this demonstrates is that, although it is convenient for administrative purposes to divide a country into a number of regions, people within those regions may identify with a smaller area within that region: one of the older counties, such as Durham, Cheshire or Essex; or a town or city, such as Sunderland, Chester or Chelmsford, or even an area within a town or city. Larger divisions are also important: people from Dundee in Scotland may identify with their fellow Scots when the 'other' is England, for instance, when national teams play each other at football or rugby, but identify with their own city when the rival is a team from Glasgow. In England, anybody from the North (a region whose boundaries are vague, as we shall see) feels an affinity with other 'Northerners' against 'the South', but there are long-standing rivalries between, for instance, Lancashire and Yorkshire, Liverpool and Manchester, Leeds and Bradford, and so on. This sense of regional identity is not confined to the UK. A proud and patriotic citizen of the US may identify him- or herself as 'Northern' or 'Southern'; as belonging to a particular state, such as Philadelphia, Georgia or Texas; to a city, such as Pittsburgh, Atlanta or Dallas, or, where the larger cities are concerned, to a district. In Australia, there is rivalry between states: players born in New South Wales and Queensland play rugby for the state in which they were born in an annual 'State of Origin' series.

When we discuss issues of language and region, then, the sense of 'region' must be fluid, covering whatever geographical areas are considered distinct from each other by the people living in them, and whatever varieties of English are perceived as different from each other by the people who speak and hear them. We may refer to 'Northern' dialects of English in England, or 'Southern' dialects of US English; we may discuss the dialects of Yorkshire or North Carolina; or we may refer to the dialects of Sheffield or Okracoke. For the purpose of this book, all of these dialects will be termed 'regional'.

The discussion in the previous section takes it for granted that 'regions', however we define them, are still distinct in countries such as the UK, the US and Australia. All these countries have various 'regional' levels of government (not to mention the separate 'national' governments of Scotland and Wales within the UK), but are these regions anything other than a political or administrative convenience? In the twenty-first century, is there still a sense that one city, county, state or region is different from the next, or are we really living in a 'global village', where every high street has the same burger chains, coffee bars and chain stores?

In recent years, many studies and articles have appeared expressing concern about the loss of local distinctiveness in 'Western' countries. The term **macdonaldisation** has been coined to describe the way in which global corporations have taken over sites formerly occupied by local companies. In the UK, a charitable organisation, Common Ground, has been set up as a pressure group to counteract this. Their website contains the following proclamation:

How then has it happened that we can stand in many high streets, factories, fields or forests and feel we could be anywhere? Why does MacDonald's force upon our high streets an idea born in corporate strategy meetings thousands of miles away? . . . Why are we planting the same trees everywhere? . . . Why does the pursuit of standards now result in standardisation. Apples, bricks, sheep and gates, all of which have had generations of careful guided evolution creating qualities related to conditions of locality and need, no longer show the differentiation which whispers rather than shouts where you are.

(www.commonground.org.uk/local.html)

Craig Taylor, writing in the *Guardian Weekend* on 23 November 2002, quotes an interviewee as saying, with reference to out-of-town shopping malls: 'These big centres, they're all the same. People don't know if they're in Düsseldorf or Vancouver.' He goes on to comment:

Unfortunately, this sense of sameness is just as much a problem for the British high street. 'Standardisation has become, over the years, a real danger', says Steve Burt, director of Stirling University's Institute for Retail Studies. 'What's the point of going to town centre B if you're going to get a carbon copy of what you had in town centre A? It's more and more likely that there will always be the same Boots and Next.'

(www.guardian.co.uk/britain/article/0,,845870,00.
html#article_continue)

The same fear is expressed in a paper by the Council for the Protection of Rural England *The Lie of the Land* in 2003:

What we are witnessing is a levelling down of England. Some landscape character loss is spectacular, such as that left in the wake of new out-of-town shopping centres or road developments. Some is more gradual. Year by year, distinctive hedgerow patterns break up and disappear as land management practices change. One by one, utility transmission masts and poles disturb treasured views. The net effect is a frightening sense that everywhere is becoming the same.

Yet there is also a sense that some places do retain their distinctiveness, and that people are still proud of their 'home' town, city or region.

5

Activity

Common Ground has produced an ABC of local distinctiveness, which is reproduced in Text 1: A Common Ground Alphabet. Try to produce an ABC for your own town, city or region, including any features that you think make it 'different' from others. If you are working in a class where all the members have lived in the same place for most of their lives, then different groups can be assigned different sections of the alphabet. If you all come from different places, you may want to choose one of these places for each group to discuss. The Common Ground alphabet includes a wide variety of 'distinctive' features, including foods such as Caerphilly cheese; festivals such as the Notting Hill Carnival; traditional customs such as Derbyshire well dressings; sporting events such as the Epsom Derby; and industrial artefacts such as the Iron Bridge in Staffordshire. You might find that local beers, such as Newcastle Brown Ale or Boddingtons, or local celebrities, mean more to you; or that local industries, such as steel in Sheffield (the 'Steel City'), coal mining in South Yorkshire, Northumberland or South Wales, or cotton in Lancashire, still resonate with local identity even after much of the industry has disappeared. If it is difficult at first to find examples of local distinctiveness, you may need to visit local libraries, museums and tourist board offices, and talk to friends and family about this. When you have produced your 'ABCs', present them to the class, and discuss whether, having thought carefully about what makes 'your' town or city distinctive, you think that this distinctiveness in under threat, and whether local distinctiveness is still important to younger people.

Text 1: A Common Ground Alphabet

> . . . **A**lder carr, ammonites **B**arns, bluebells, beck, backlane, the Bronte sisters, bridge, Black Dog, beech hedge, badger sett **C**ream teas, chalk-figures, chine, Constable, carnival, church bells, cooling towers, chicory, commons, Collywestons, crinkle-crankle wall **D**rystone walls, dewpond, Dorset Horn **E**lgar, English bond, **F**en, flint, field-names, fells, foghorn **G**asometer, gospel oak, glowworm **H**ousemartins, hopfield, hombeam, harbour, hillfort, haymeadow, heath, Hook Norton **I**nn sign, islands **J**ack O Kent, jackdaws **K**ent cobs, kingfisher, kilns **L**ong barrow, lichen, Lambton Worm, lighting, level crossing, lapwings **M**ay Day, milestone, mazzard, mine, mosque, may bug, market place, March hare **N**orfolk beefing, newts, Northumbrian pipes **O**ast house, Old Man's Beard, orchard **P**it tip, pier, pargetting, pollarded willows, pillbox **Q**uarry, quay, quicksand **R**ain, red soil, ridgeway, Robin Hood, rookery **S**nottygogs, sand dunes, Staffordshire blues, stilton, stile, shopfront, spire, slate, steelworks, starlings, shingles, stargazy pie **T**amworths, tottergrass, twitchel, tarn, tump, Tan Hill Fair **U**ndercliff **V**alerian, viaduct **W**atercress beds, weather-board, well-dressing, walkmill, winterbourne, wind turbines, wold, wild raspberries **Y**ew **Z**awns . . .

(www.england-in-particular.info)

(There is no commentary for this activity.)

So far, we have been discussing regional distinctiveness and regional identity with little reference to language. However, there is a clear link between regions that are distinct from other regions and the dialects spoken in those regions. In England, many nicknames for people from certain cities or regions also refer to the dialects of those places: *Cockney* was first used to refer to citizens of London in 1600, according to the *OED*. An early quotation that illustrates this use is: 'Londiners, and all within the sound of Bow-bell, are in reproch called Cocknies' (1617). By the eighteenth century, the word was also being used to describe the dialect of lower-class Londoners, again, usually 'in reproach'. George Campbell in his *Philosophy of Rhetoric* (1776) refers to 'an idiom of the Cockney language', and John Walker in 1791, warns his readers to avoid the faults of his 'countrymen, the Cockneys', such as dropping the 'h' from words such as *house* and using 'v' for 'w' and *vice versa*. *Scouse* was originally the name of a stew (and still is), but the *OED* records the term used for a native of Liverpool in 1945, and for the dialect in 1963:

> 1945 *Southern Daily Echo* 27 Dec. 4/3 He was stopped by his Lordship and asked to explain the meaning of three words 'oppo', 'Geordie' and 'scouse'. His interpretations were: 'oppo' slang for opposite number, friend or colleague, 'Geordie', a native of Newcastle-upon-Tyne; 'scouse', a native of Liverpool where they eat 'scouse' (stew).

> 1963 *Guardian* 3 June 10/5 This rock group suddenly made Liverpool fashionable in the entertainment world. After their first two records it became necessary for people in the business in London to learn a few words of Scouse.

The context of the 1945 quotation, in which a judge requires explanations of the **slang** terms used by a defendant or witness, suggests that the term was in use earlier, but, as the date suggests, it was in the Second World War that servicemen from different parts of the UK served and fought together, and so developed and disseminated nicknames for each other. *Geordie* had been in use for longer, shown by the *OED* records from 1866: 'The sailors belonging to the ports of the North Eastern coast of England are called Jordies', but *Brummie*, referring to citizens of Birmingham, is first recorded in 1941: 'You're a Brummy boy. I can tell by your accent.' Far from disappearing due to loss of regional distinctiveness, these terms for citizens of particular towns or cities seem to have been multiplying in the late twentieth and early twenty-first centuries.

The *OED* does not record *Mackem* (Sunderland), *Smoggie* (Middlesbrough/ Teesside), *Pie-eater* (Wigan) or *Manc* (Manchester), but they can all be found in fanzines and on websites such as the *Urban Dictionary* (www. urbandictionary.com). The entry for *Smoggie* reads as follows:

> A person originating from Teesside, North East England, particu-larly Middlesbrough and Stockton, usually an avid fan of Premier League side Middlesbrough Football [Club], and the God that is Juninho. *Geordie* and *Mackam* [*sic*] haters, and so called because of the Smog produced by the I.C.I. chemical plant. Shortened from original nickname of 'Smog monster'.
>
> (www.urbandictionary.com)

These terms usually begin as insults aimed at one group of people by those from a rival town or city, often, as in the above definition, in the context of sporting rivalry. However, since *Scousers, Geordies, Mackems* and *Smoggies* tend to be proud of 'belonging' to their town or city, they accept and adopt the term in due course. Some of these terms actually refer to distinctive elements of the local dialect: *Mackem* comes from the pronun-ciation of *make* as /mak/ still heard in Sunderland, and other terms based on dialect features include *Yinsers* for citizens of Pittsburgh, so called because they use *yins* as a plural form of *you*; *Hoi Toiders* for people from the Outer Banks, North Carolina, who pronounce *high* as /hoi/ and so on; *Dee-dahs*, used by people from Barnsley to refer to Sheffielders, who pro-nounced *thee* and *thou* as /di:/ and /da:/; and *Seestus*, referring to citizens of Paisley in Scotland, who used to begin sentences with 'seestu' ('do you see?'). In many cases, the dialect features referred to in the nicknames have all but disappeared from modern usage, but the nickname has stuck. All this suggests that local identity is as important as ever, and that dialect is one of the most important markers of this identity.

Even when a feature of local dialect is disappearing, it may be preserved in a restricted range of words, or in particular contexts, often those that are associated with local identity. The pronunciation [u:] in words such as *house, now, town*, etc. is **recessive** in Tyneside, but is widely used in a few words, notably *Toon* meaning, not any old town, but Newcastle, or, increasingly, Newcastle United Football Club. A similar phenomenon exists in Cardiff, where the stigmatised 'Cardiff *a*' is found in all words in the **phrase** *Cardiff Arms Park*, (the former rugby stadium, now replaced by the Millennium Stadium) and in the name of a local beer *Brain's Dark*. It is interesting that the words that preserve these local pronunciations are those that refer to the cities themselves and to local icons. As Nikolas Coupland writes, referring to the 'Cardiff *a*': 'regional pronunciation and local experience have a mutually encouraging, we might say symbiotic, relationship' (1988: 27).

Of course, regional identity is not static, especially in societies where young people in particular are mobile. Carmen Llamas (2000) investigated variation and change in the dialect of Middlesbrough. One area which showed complex patterns of variation was the pronunciation of /p/, /t/, and /k/. The younger speakers, especially the young women, tended to use the **glottalised** pronunciations of these **consonants** more than the older people did. Since these glottalised pronunciations are normally associated with the **accent** of Tyneside ('Geordie'), Llamas suggests that the speech of younger females in particular may be **converging** with that of 'further north in Tyneside, Wearside and Durham' and **diverging** from 'the standard British English unmarked variant, but also... from realisations found further south in Yorkshire' (2000: 137). Using an Identification Questionnaire which asked questions about attitudes to the local accent and the area, Llamas found that, while older people identified themselves as coming from Yorkshire (Middlesbrough was in Yorkshire until 1968), younger people identified with 'the North-East'. Although these young people expressed a strong hostility towards the idea of being identified as 'Geordie', they did wish to be identified as 'North Eastern' or, more specifically, Middlesbrough. Llamas explains this as follows:

> The most plausible interpretation of the increased use of the glottalised stops . . . seems to be that in increasing their use of a localised feature, young speakers from Middlesbrough are not identifying with Newcastle, but are indexing their Middlesbrough identity.
>
> (2000: 143)

We shall see in the next unit how features of accent and dialect that are identified with a certain town, city or region are used in various kinds of text, often for humorous purposes, but also to express solidarity with other speakers of those accents and dialects.

Activity

As part of her research into accent and identity in Middlesbrough, Carmen Llamas devised a questionnaire from which she could measure the extent to which people identify with their home town or city. This questionnaire has since been modified and used in other towns and cities. The questionnaire shown in Text 2: Identity Questionnaire has been designed for use anywhere. Answer the questions yourself and then compare your answers with those given by other people in your class.

Text 2: Identity Questionnaire

Form ID No. (_____/_____/_____/_____)

Identity Questionnaire

1. Is there a name for people from your town or city (such as *Scouser* for Liverpool or *Geordie* for Newcastle? If so, would you use this name to describe yourself?
   ....

2. What accent do you think you have?
   ....

3. Is your accent different from the accent of nearby towns or cities? Can you think of any specific ways in which it is different? For instance, are there any words which are pronounced differently?
   ....
   ....

4. Are you proud of your accent or would you rather not have any accent at all?
   ....

5. Would you prefer to have a different accent? If so, which one? Why?
   ....

6. Do you think it is good to have an accent? Why or why not?
   ....

7. Have you ever felt embarrassed about your accent? When? Why?
   ....

8. Are there different accents in your region? If there are, what are they? Do you like them? Can you tell them apart easily?
   ....
   ....

9. Where do you like going in your spare time within your region? What is your favourite shopping centre?
   ....

10. What football or other sports team do you mainly support? Who is its main rival?
    ....

11. What do you think of your home town or city?
    ....

12. Do you think that another nearby town or city is more favoured than yours, and because of that it tends to get the best facilities? Why or why not?
    ....

13. In which town or city are people generally more friendly? Why?
    ....

14. Is it necessary to speak with a local accent to 'belong' to your town or city?
    ....

15. What are the main reasons for any rivalry between your town or city and any of its neighbours?
    ....
    ....

Commentary

1   As we have seen, many terms for people from a certain town or city
    begin as insults, but then become a badge of pride. Some people
    are very proud to call themselves by these names, others less so.
    Younger people, especially those thinking of going away to university,
    might feel less attached to their home town, and might even think
    of these names as 'old-fashioned', or referring to people different from
    themselves.

2   A **broad** accent is often associated with local identity. Are those who
    feel proud of the name associated with the town or city also those
    who think they speak with the local accent?

3   Local accents and dialects are often thought to be different from each
    other even when the distance between the two places is small. In such
    cases, local people can usually identify a word or expression that marks
    out people from the 'other' place.

4   Some people are ashamed of their local accents, and feel they would
    get better jobs, etc. if they 'did not have an accent'. If any of your
    class feel this, are they the ones who don't identify strongly with their
    home town or city in other ways?

5   As we shall see in Unit three, some accents are thought to be more
    attractive than others. Do you, or any of your class, think that you
    would like a different regional accent?

6   This question follows on from 4 and 5, exploring attitudes to local
    accents more generally.

7   People who speak with a local accent have often experienced preju-
    dice, or misunderstanding, especially if they have moved to a different
    part of the country. These experiences are not easily forgotten: I can
    still remember being teased about my accent when I went to univer-
    sity over 30 years ago.

8   Like 3, this question aims to discover the features of local accents that
    distinguish speakers from neighbouring places.

9   This question aims to find out where people, especially young people,
    are likely to come into contact with speakers of a different dialect,
    and whether they might be influenced by this. If you live in a smaller

town, but go shopping or clubbing in a larger city, that may influence your dialect. Centres such as Newcastle, Manchester and Leeds draw in people from a wide area, and the 'dialect levelling' that has been observed may be caused by these major cities influencing the speech of those who go there for leisure.

10   This may seem trivial, but, as Carmen Llamas found, local rivalry is expressed most keenly in the context of sport, especially football, where the 'derby' match allows supporters to indulge in banter with their neighbours. She found that the change in identity, whereby younger people in Middlesbrough saw themselves as 'North Eastern' rather than 'Yorkshire', but resisted being identified as 'Geordies', was echoed by their choice of Newcastle United rather than Leeds as the major local rival in football.

11   This is an open-ended question, designed to find out whether people are proud or ashamed of their home town or city, or indifferent, and what the reasons for this might be.

12   This question deals with local rivalries: people from a smaller town or city often see their larger neighbour as favoured.

13   This is intended to discover whether people feel positive about their own town or city: do they think people are friendlier there?

14   This question returns to the matter of accent and identity: can you, for instance, be a Scouser if you don't have a Scouse accent?

15   The last question returns to the matter of local rivalry. This is important, because we often identify ourselves in terms of what we are not just as much as what we are. Liverpool is different from Manchester, the North from the South, Scotland from England, etc.

SUMMARY

This unit has looked at definitions of region and at issues of regional diversity and distinctiveness. Although there is concern about 'macdonaldisation', many towns, cities and regions retain various features that make them different from others. Use of local dialect is one way of expressing this distinctiveness.

Extension

1 Research the way that your town, city or region is presented in tourist literature, museums and visitor attractions. What features are high-lighted as making this place distinctive? Do these have any importance for people who live there, or are they just for tourists or visitors?

2 Discuss changes in your town, city or region with people who have lived there for a long time. Have they noticed the place becoming less distinctive, for instance with the loss of local businesses from the high street?

Regional language and its uses

We saw in Unit one how regional and local identity are still important to us in the twenty-first century, even, or especially, when every high street in Britain or even the world, has the same coffee shops, chain stores and fast-food outlets. This tendency for towns and cities in the developed world to be dominated by the same global companies is known, for obvious reasons as macdonaldisation. Some commentators see a similar process threatening the diversity of regional dialects of English, as features from **Estuary English** spread throughout Britain, and American English exerts its influence worldwide. There have been many articles in newspapers, as well as more academic papers, about the spread of 'Estuary' features such as the glottal stop pronunciation of the /t/ in *butter*, *water*, etc. to most of Britain, and of 'American' features such as the use of *like* and *so* in, for example, the trailer for the final series of *Friends*: 'It's like, so the last series!' These articles give the impression that regional dialects are endangered species, unable to live alongside 'Estuary' and American English just as red squirrels cannot survive in the company of grey ones. However, examples of regional English are not hard to find: texts in dialect can be found on the web, in souvenir shops and tourist offices and in regional newspapers, while regional accents are often used in soap operas such as *Coronation Street*, *EastEnders* and *Emmerdale*, where the locality of the setting is important, and in advertisements where the product is associated with a region, such as Ambrosia Creamed Rice ('ooh aarh, it's Ambrosia'), and Boddingtons

Beer (formerly brewed in Manchester). In this unit, we will look at some examples of regional language and discuss the ways in which the language of these texts differs from **Standard English**, the intended readership, and the motivation and assumptions of the authors.

Activity

Look at Text 3: Word for Northerners, which I received as an e-mail attachment from a relative, but which is posted on several websites, including that of UK Technical Support www.uktsupport.co.uk/. This is a **parody**, or 'spoof' version, of an advertisement for new software to support Microsoft Word. There are many versions of this, including 'Word for Geordies', 'Australian Word' and versions for Newfoundland, for Canada and for the Southern states of the US.

Prepare some notes for a commentary, using the framework for analysis provided. First look at the internal aspects, the technical features of the language used, then consider the external features.

Framework for analysis

Internal aspects
• What regional vocabulary is used in the text?
• What spellings are used in the text to indicate regional pronunciation (accent)?
• What features of grammar in the text are regional or **non-standard**?
• What is interesting about the design of the text, its **graphology**?

External aspects
• Who is writing the text?
• For what purpose are they writing the text?
• For what audience are they writing the text?
• What is the text's level of formality?
• What attitudes, values and assumptions are in the text?
• What kind of text are they producing?

All of the above form part of the *context* of the text.

(This is an edited version of *A Framework for Looking at Texts*, published by LINC in *Language in the National Curriculum*, p. 84)

Text 3: Word for Northerners

It's Grim Up North!

Relocating in Northern England is good for business; lots of the starving unemployed eager to work for a pittance of pay and daring not to complain or they'll be out on the street with their dozens of screaming bairns, and their benefits cut for six months.

But are you really getting the most from them?

Are they 'as much use as a chocolate teapot' when it comes to the complexities of modern technology?

Research has shown that Northerners **aren't as thick as they make out**. They just can't grasp the meaning of modern English.

That's why you need our **new** software package . . .

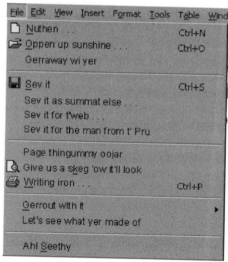**Word for Northerners!**

The installation process automatically modifies their Windows start button

All the usual Word menu option are there, but in a language your Northern England employees can understand

File Edit View Insert Format Tools Table Wind	
Nuthen . . .	Ctrl+N
Oppen up sunshine . . .	Ctrl+O
Gerraway wi yer	
Sev it	Ctrl+S
Sev it as summat else . . .	
Sev it for t'web . . .	
Sev it for the man from t' Pru	
Page thingummy oojar	
Give us a skeg 'ow it'll look	
Writing iron . . .	Ctrl+P
Gerrout with it	▶
Let's see what yer made of	
Ahl Seethy	

Even the warning messages have changed

And if all else fails, they will have a help facility that folks from Barnsley and Bradford can understand

So what are you waiting for? Me to go to the foot of our stair?!

Buy your employees Northern Word today, and see your profits rise!

For **this month only** we'll ship Northern Word to you for the incredibly daft price of

Only £59.99 +VAT !

Tha'd 'ave t'be soft in t'head not to say "Aye, champion!"

And that's not all!

Respond to this advert within 10 days and receive free:

Great New Translating Tool!

With this little beauty you can have your employees type in their own language:

Ow do youth, 'ows tha bin?

A mun tell thee that t'clever sods 'ere at Hardwick and Granville 'ave cum oop wi this reet grand gubbins wot can 'elp thee a treet. Its sorta like this great whopping oojah wi' flashing lights an' knobs on an' all wot can do thee addin up faster than thar can spit on a whippet. An' that's saying summat!
If tha wants a skeg then get thee arse over t' Wool Exchange on Mundy where wil be showing t'bugga off.
If thars a jammy sod then 'appen thar'l even win a prize, so who sez tha dunt get owt for nowt in this world?!

Ah'll sithee then youth,

John Northerner
Bloke wot does t'marketing

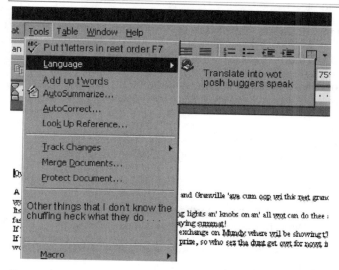

At a touch of a key Northern Word can convert it into **proper English**.

Et Voilà!

Dear Mr Customer,

Announcing the new Accounts software from H&G Systems Ltd!

Come along to our stand at the NEC this Monday and see it for yourself!

Enter your business card into the lucky draw for a chance to win a great prize!

Hope to see you there,

John Southerner
Marketing Executive

With this piece of clever software your customers **need never even know** that you are exploiting a demoralised workforce of ex-miners and ex-shipyard welders desperate to work for your pitiful barely legal wages!

And **you'll** make a killing!

For further details, e-mail northernword@patronisingmanagers.com

Testimonial

But don't just take our word for it.

Here are some of the great things people have been sayimg about Northern Word:

> "Before we installed Northern Word onto the PC's of all our journalists, no-one outside of the West Riding of Yorkshire would buy our paper. Now even Saath Landoners can understand it!" *Editor, Telegraph & Argus*

> "Thank you for creating such an excellent product! Now my employees can use Northern Word to write out their CV's, as I am making them all redundant next week!" *Manager, Bastard & Greedy Ltd*

> "Phew, what a God-send! Now I can dismiss all the monkeys working in our typing pool, and employ Northerners instead at a much cheaper rate!" *N.Other Manager, Screwthepoor & Sons*

> "Is't tha tekking piss or summat? Ah'll come ovar there and give thee such a clout that <cut>" *Fred Hardwhaite, Northerner*

Don't delay!

Buy Northern Word Today!

(www.uktsupport.co.uk/humour/wordfornortherners.pdf)

An internal approach to the study of language involves the analysis of spellings, words and grammar. Where the object of study is dialect or regional language, we concentrate on the features that mark the text out as 'non-standard', or different from the Standard English that we usually find in written texts. As it has been normal practice to use Standard English at least in printed texts in England since the sixteenth century, any author writing in dialect is doing so for a specific purpose. We need to look at external aspects of the text to understand why the writer is doing this and what effect he or she intends to create.

Looking first at the internal aspects, there are several words that may be unfamiliar to readers from outside the 'North', or at least are easily identified as non-standard. The first sentence is written mainly in Standard English, but contains the Northern word *bairns* meaning 'children' in the phrase 'dozens of screaming bairns'. The Northern word here helps to evoke the contrast between the large, unruly families of working-class Northerners and the 2.4 children of respectable, middle-class Southerners.

One word which readers outside the 'North' or even Yorkshire, might not recognise, is *skeg* in 'Give us a skeg 'ow it'll look'. *Skeg* obviously means 'glance', and the spelling with /sk/ suggests that it is one of many words of Norse origin found in Yorkshire dialects as a consequence of the Viking settlements in this area. *Gubbins* is labelled as 'obsolete' in the *OED* and as meaning 'fragments of fish'. Here, the meaning has been extended to 'bits' of anything, and eventually to a word that, like *oojah*, just means 'thingy'. Regional dialects often preserve words that have died out in Standard English, and *gubbins* is one of these.

Other words in Text 3: Word for Northerners are used more widely throughout the North: *aye, nay, owt, nowt* and *summat* are used for Standard English *yes, no, anything, nothing* and *something*. The terms for *hello* and *goodbye* are *'ow do, 'ey up* and *seethy* (I'll see thee), and *champion* is used to express pleasure and agreement: 'Tha'd 'ave to be soft in t'ead not to say "Aye, champion!".' *Grand* is used in the Northern sense of 'good' rather than 'majestic' and *reet* ('right') for *very* or *really*.

Swear words are used quite frequently throughout Text 3. Obviously, swearing is neither confined to dialect, nor used by all speakers of dialect, but here it adds to the impression of the down-to-earth Northerner. The swear words are milder than in other dialect versions of Word, though: there is only one *What the fuks that*, with other swear words such as *arse, bastard, bugga* (*bugger*, not really considered a swear word in the North), *sods* and *tekkin piss*. There is even one Northern (more specifically, Yorkshire) term used to avoid swearing: *chuffing heck*.

Dialect tends to be used in informal circumstances, when talking to people with whom the speaker is familiar, so **terms of endearment** are frequently used. Here we find *love, sunshine* and *youth*, all of which are used as familiar terms of address in parts of the North. They are amusing here because we do not expect to be addressed in this way by the anonymous author of a software package, but they evoke the 'homely' image of the North.

As well as individual words, there are a number of phrases and **sayings** that are characteristically Northern in Text 3. The heading 'It's grim up North!' is a well-known cliché about the 'North–South divide' in England, used to describe the grimy industrial towns depicted in films of the 1950s and 1960s. This is so well known that recent newspaper articles commenting on the regeneration of Northern cities and the overcrowding in the South are headed 'It's grim down South!'. 'Sev it for t'man from t'Pru', refers to the saying 'Save it for the man from the Pru(dential)', referring to the company which provided easy credit for cash-strapped Northerners, while 'What are you waiting for? Me to go to the foot of our stair?' is a reference to a Northern expression of surprise 'Well, I'll go to the foot of our stair!'.

One of the most obvious markers of regional language today is accent. When we use the term accent, we are referring to pronunciation only, not vocabulary or grammar. I am writing this sentence in Standard English: none of the words are dialect words, and the grammar is standard, but if I were to read it out loud, you would be able to tell where I was born (within about 50 miles) because of my accent. Because 'Word for Northerners' is a written text, the author has had to use **semi-phonetic spelling** to indicate some of the features of a Northern accent. Linguists use the more accurate international phonetic alphabet (IPA) (see pp. 103–104) to indicate the precise sounds of an accent, but authors writing for the general public use non-standard spellings as a guide. There is a general level of agreement about the conventions of semi-phonetic spelling, so it is usually not too difficult to work out how the text is meant to sound. In any case, the intention is to indicate the most well-known, stereotypical features of the accent rather than a full and precise representation. We shall see in Unit seven that semi-phonetic spelling is widely used in dialect literature.

The start button in 'Word for Northerners' is marked *gerron withit*. Here, the use of <rr> for <t> indicates the pronunciation, used very widely throughout the North and Midlands of England, in which a <t> followed by a vowel is pronounced as <r>. We see this again in *gerraway wi yer*. 'H-dropping', a feature that is neither confined to the North, nor found in all parts of the North (Geordies, for instance, pronounce the <h>), is indicated by the use of an apostrophe to indicate that the <h> is missing: *'ow, 'ome, 'ere* and *'appen* are all examples of this.*

---

* Throughout this book, angled brackets < > are used to mark spellings, and diagonals / / or square brackets [ ] to mark sounds. Words in capitals, e.g. CAR, are keywords (*see* p. 103).

The vowels of Northern accents are very different to those of the South, and various conventions are used to signal this. In standard spelling, a double consonant often indicates that the vowel before is short: thus *matter, barrier* as opposed to *mate, bare*. Here, the spelling *oppen* suggests a short 'o', as in *hot*, while in *sev, med* the use of <e> instead of <a> and missing out the final <e> of standard *save, made*, signal the Northern pronunciations with the 'e' of *kept*. *Nah then* has the spelling <ah> to indicate the long 'a' of *car* rather than the 'ow' of *out*, and the <oo> of *oop* is a conventional way of representing the 'broad' Northern 'u' used in words such as *cup* as well as *good*.

Apart from spellings such as these, which attempt to indicate Northern pronunciations, the writer also uses **eye-dialect**. This is a term used to describe cases where the spelling is non-standard, but the pronunciation indicated by the spelling is not. *Sez* and *wot* both suggest pronunciations which would be used throughout England, and by the 'poshest' speakers, but the non-standard spelling adds to the impression of informality.

There are also several instances of the use of regional grammar in Text 3. The most obvious 'Northern' feature is the use of <t'> for Standard English *the*. Examples are *Sev it for t'web, t'changes thaz made, bloke wot does t'marketing*. In one case *Is tha tekkin piss*, the 'the' is missed out altogether. In most of Lancashire and Yorkshire, this pattern, in which 'the' is sometimes reduced to a glottal stop, and sometimes missed out completely, is still found. In *Sev it for the man from t'Pru* there is one example of 'the' left in its full form. This looks inconsistent, but in fact most speakers in these areas would use 'the' sometimes.

A more 'old-fashioned' Northern feature is the use of *thee, thy* and *thar* for *you* and *your*. *Thee* and *thou* were used in earlier English, much as *tu* in French, and *du* in German, to address someone either inferior to, or very well known to, the speaker. This went out of use in Standard English around 1700, but it is still found in some dialects. There are speakers in Lancashire and Yorkshire who still use *thee* and *thou*: in Sheffield there is even a term *thee-ing and tha-ing* meaning to use broad dialect, but most younger people would claim not to use them now.

Dunt for 'doesn't' shows a grammatical pattern used in Lancashire and Yorkshire, where the consonant before the <n> in a negative verb is missed out. Thus *isn't* would be *int*, *wouldn't* becomes *wunt*, etc.

I commented above on the use of eye-dialect in *wot*: in 'Bloke wot does t'marketing' the *wot* also indicates non-standard grammatical usage. The **relative pronoun** 'who' is not used here, with 'wot' ('what') being used instead. This is typical of a wide range of non-standard dialects of English, in which *who, whom* and *which* are rarely used.

The graphology of Text 3 mimics that of Microsoft Word very closely. Buttons and icons are exactly the same as those that appear in the standard program. I have known people to be fooled by this, and most frustrated when they click on the icons and nothing happens! Obviously, this use of graphology is an important part of the parody: the familiar icons contrast with the unexpected use of Northern dialect.

Overall, Text 3 has a number of features that indicate non-standard, and more specifically, Northern, dialect. These are found in the parts claiming to be instructions within 'Word for Northerners': the introduction and commentary are in Standard English, the language 'wot posh buggers speak'. The features of Northern English used are:

◎ dialect vocabulary such as *bairns*, *gubbins*, *skeg*;

◎ Northern phrases and sayings;

◎ semi-phonetic spelling to indicate accent;

◎ features of non-standard grammar.

Clearly, somebody has gone to a great deal of trouble to construct a clever parody of the Microsoft house style. In considering the external aspects of Text 3, we can come to an understanding of why it was written and how it works.

The first question in the external aspects section of the framework on p. 16, 'who is writing the text?' is impossible to answer when the text has been transmitted in the way that 'Word for Northerners' was. Web-users receive texts like this from friends, who in turn received them from other friends, and the originator is often anonymous. Finding the author of a web-transmitted joke is as impossible as finding the 'friend of a friend' whose dead granny really was brought home from Spain on the roof rack of the family car, or who really picked up the phantom hitchhiker. However, we can infer several things about the author: he or she is certainly computer-literate and very familiar with the products of Microsoft. The level of detail in the representation of dialect suggests that he or she is probably a Northerner, and references in the text to Barnsley, Bradford and West Yorkshire, as well as many of the linguistic details, point to Yorkshire rather than, for instance, Newcastle. The text is posted on a website that gives technical advice, but there is no claim to authorship here.

The intended audience is likewise made up of web-users who are computer-literate and familiar with the Microsoft house style. To understand the joke fully, they would also need to be familiar with Northern English and the cultural stereotypes associated with it.

The **genre** of Text 3 has already been alluded to: it is clearly an example of parody, a genre in which a text closely follows the style of another well-known text, but alters it in ways that are humorous. Thus, comedy films such as *Scream* and *Shaun of the Dead* are funny because they use the well-known conventions of horror, but introduce subtle changes that create humour rather than fear. In 'Word for Northerners' the language outside the spoof program is that of marketing: propositions are put to the reader that seem intended to persuade him or her to buy. Questions such as 'Are you really getting the most from them?' and the use of the second **person** to address the reader directly, along with the use of bold typeface and exclamation marks for emphasis, are all techniques used in advertising. Technical vocabulary such as 'installation processes', 'the usual Word menu options', suggests that author and reader are equally familiar with computer **jargon**, and superior to the Northerners who, however, 'aren't as thick as they make out'. This creates an illusion that the *purpose* of Text 3 is to sell a new software package to employers in the North, but only the most naive reader would fail to recognise the true purpose as, simply, an elaborate joke.

In a parody, there are always at least two levels of meaning: that on the surface, which points towards the genre being parodied, and that below, which points away from this and reveals the joke. If we consider the levels of formality, on one level we have a mixture of the fairly informal language of advertising, with direct address to the reader and contracted forms of verbs such as 'aren't' and 'we'll' and the more formal, technical language of computing. This would be in keeping with an advertisement for a software package, but the language within the spoof program is extremely informal, using familiar terms of address ('thou'), swear words and homely sayings more at home in a soap opera. The contrast exposes Text 3 as a parody and creates the humour.

The attitudes and assumptions hinted at in Text 3 likewise operate on two levels. On the surface, the assumption is that the North is a post-industrial wasteland populated by 'ex-miners and shipyard welders' and their 'dozens of screaming bairns' with no choice but to be exploited by 'greedy bastard' managers from the South. This 'grim up North' stereotype has been portrayed in films such as *The Full Monty* and *Brassed Off*, to mixed reactions from Northerners. Postings on a weblog on which 'Word for Northerners' is discussed likewise express a range of reactions: 'Nigel' writes: 'Speaking as a northener [*sic*] who's an editor, and former journalist and copywriter, I'd just like to say: farts to this', whereas 'Gert' seems to get the joke, and replies: 'By 'eck Nigel, you're so right. Look, our kid, I'm just a thick northerner who can't cope under pressure.' What makes 'Word for

Northerners' amusing is that the stereotypes do not carry the values of the author or most of the readers: texts like this operate as 'in jokes' in which, in this case, sophisticated, computer-literate Northerners collude in laughing at the outdated stereotypes still commonly used in the media. The author and readers of Text 3 are not redundant ex-miners, or, if they are, they have probably retrained and begun successful second careers in information technology. If readers from outside the North still believe that it's 'grim', then the joke is on them.

Another assumption embodied in Text 3 is more straightforward, because the writer is probably less conscious of it: 'the North' seems to be confined to Yorkshire. The dialect portrayed is that of West Yorkshire, and place names referred to are likewise all in this area. Some postings on the weblog cited above take up this point: 'Gordon' writes:

'Wow that's really far North, Bradford, Barnsley? Why it's positively Arctic!! (Sorry obvious rant from a Scot.)'

and 'Bel' posts the following:

I've nearly finished reading Sons & Lovers. You may be surprised to learn that DH Lawrence wrote his novel using Word for Northerners, despite the fact that it was set in and around Nottingham, which is, in my opinion, the Midlands.

We saw in Unit one that regional divisions such as the 'North' are not objectively defined: to a Geordie, Nottingham is in the Midlands, while, to a Londoner, it is in the North.

Activity

Using the framework for analysis on p. 16, prepare a commentary on Text 4: Pittsburgh T-shirt, which appears on a T-shirt sold as a souvenir in Pittsburgh, USA. Once again, you should consider both the internal and external features of this text. As the text consists of individual words, you should look some of these up in the *OED Online* to discover their origins.

Text 4: Pittsburgh T-shirt

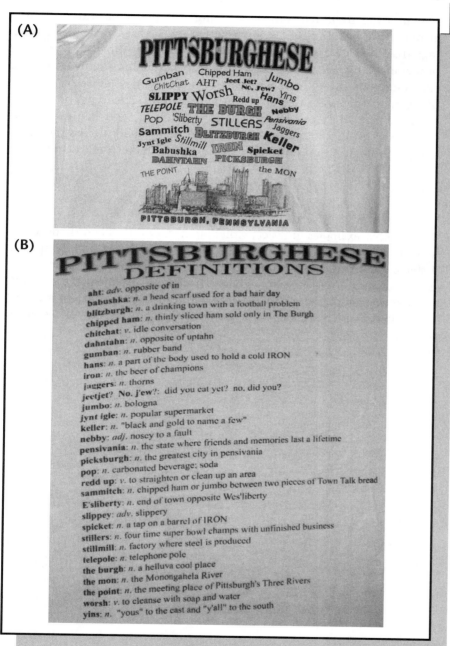

(See the commentary on p. 91.)

SUMMARY

This unit has indicated some of the linguistic areas that can be looked at under the headings of 'regional language', such as vocabulary, spellings that indicate accent, and grammar. It has also shown how the use of regional language can be put to use in constructing sophisticated and elaborate texts, which convey layers of meaning and ideology. The use of regional language is tied up with the prevailing stereotypes of regional speakers that affect our judgement of individuals, and in turn can be exploited for humour, advertising or tourism. We will discuss the social and psychological implications of these stereotypes further in Unit three.

Extension

Collect other examples of dialect writing from tourist sites and shops, either in your own city or elsewhere. These can be small books and pamphlets, T-shirts, postcards, even mugs, tea-towels and mouse-mats. Discuss the extent to which these use semi-phonetic spelling to 'exaggerate' the dialect, or whether they present genuinely regional words. To what extent is dialect being used as a commodity here, a way of 'selling' the city or region to tourists?

Attitudes to regional language

We saw in Unit two that there are generally recognised stereotypical attitudes to certain accents and dialects, which can be evoked for humorous purposes in texts such as 'Word for Northerners' (Text 3, p. 17). In this unit, we will discuss research that has been carried out into listeners' reactions to accents, and the ways in which attitudes to regional accents have changed in the course of the twentieth and early twenty-first centuries.

In 1967, K.T. Strongman and J. Woosley published the results of an experiment that they had carried out on listeners' reactions to a range of British accents. They found that there was a very consistent pattern to their subjects' evaluation of these accents: **Received Pronunciation** (RP), the prestigious accent of British (or rather, English) English, was judged most favourably, the accents of industrial cities such as Birmingham were judged least favourably, and those of rural areas such as Cornwall were in between. They concluded that listeners' responses were drawing upon stereotypes, whereby RP was associated with intelligence, but the accents of cities such as Birmingham were linked with negative images of grimy, industrial cities and blue-collar jobs. The 'rural' accents evoked positive images of beautiful landscapes, but the inhabitants of such areas were judged likely to be unintelligent 'peasants', so their accents had both positive and negative connotations.

Drawing on this study, the social psychologist Howard Giles conducted a number of studies from the 1970s onwards, using an experimental technique devised by Lambert, Hodgson, Gardner and Fillenbaum in 1960, and known as the **matched guise** technique. This involves a speaker, usually an actor, being recorded reading the same passage in a number of different accents, or 'guises'. The same speaker is used so that listeners' reactions are not based on features that might be unique to an individual speaker, such as 'tone of voice', but the listeners are led to believe that they are hearing a number of different people. The listeners are then asked to evaluate each 'guise' on a range of attributes, such as intelligence, honesty, friendliness, etc. The results of such experiments were very consistent: the RP guise was always given the highest score for features such as intelligence, whereas regional accented guises scored higher for features such as friendliness and honesty. The same hierarchy emerged in these experiments as in Strongman and Woosley's: the urban accents of, for example, Liverpool and Birmingham were less positively evaluated than rural accents.

Research into stereotypical reactions to accents is by no means confined to Britain: indeed, Lambert first used the matched guise technique to investigate attitudes to speakers of French and English in Canada. William Labov used what he called **subjective reaction tests** to discover whether there was a common reaction among New Yorkers to pronunciations of words such as *car*, *cards*, *heart* and *morning* with and without the /r/ being pronounced. In the traditional accent of New York City, the /r/ is silent, and pronunciations such as /boid/ for *bird* are stereotypical, but, since the Second World War, the General American pronunciation with /r/ has become more common. Rather than use an actor speaking in several guises, Labov took extracts from the speech of a number of 'real' people, in some of which they pronounced /r/ consistently, while in others they pronounced at least one word without /r/. He asked listeners to imagine themselves as personnel officers, and to judge what job each 'speaker' would be suitable for. The jobs were ranked in the following order (high to low prestige): television personality, executive secretary, receptionist, switchboard operator, salesgirl, factory worker, none of these. He found that listeners consistently rated the 'r-less' guise one or two ranks lower than the 'r-full' guise for each speaker. Labov concluded from this that New Yorkers, or members of the New York **speech community** shared the same evaluation of the **variable** /r/ and that the pronunciation of words with or without /r/ evoked the same stereotyped reaction from all members of this community, whether they pronounced the /r/ themselves or not. By playing short (12–14-word) extracts of speech in which the same variable was repeated, Labov ensured that the listeners focused on this one variable rather than the accent as a whole, and was thus also able to prove that /r/ is a **salient** variable in New York, that is, one which people notice and associate with the accent.

If, as Labov proved, listeners playing the role of personnel manager consistently assign speakers using 'regional' accents or accent features to low-prestige occupations, does this have consequences in the 'real world'? In countries such as the UK and the US that have legislation to outlaw discrimination against job applicants on the grounds of age, disability, gender, race and sexual orientation, is 'accentism' still rife? In the US, there is now a lucrative business in 'accent-reduction' programmes, designed to help speakers, particularly those with 'foreign' accents, to conform to the acceptable norm of General American speech. More recently, these programmes have sprung up in the UK, but here the focus is on elimination or reduction of regional accents. The website of F. Parkes Associates has a section of questions and answers including the following:

Q. What type of people come to you for speech lessons?
A. Many people feel that their strong regional or national accent makes it difficult for others to understand them. This can apply equally to their business and social life. Many of my clients are business and professional people who want to be able to give the right impression at important meetings by speaking clearly.

(www.makethemostofyourvoice.com/)

The 'testimonials' section of the website includes an extract from an article in the *Guardian*'s 'Jobs and Money' section, January 2004:

Jenni Hunt, a lawyer from Wimbledon, and originally for Workshop [*sic*.]* used to speak with a south Yorkshire accent. But after leaving her hometown 16 years ago, she says she ditched her twang. 'I wanted to be taken seriously and to take myself seriously. I am pretty sure that it has helped my career,' she says. In an attempt to boost her other career performing voiceovers, she is having one-to-one sessions with Frances Parkes, a speech coach, and head of www.makethemostofyourvoice.com 'When I ring up agents I speak with my lawyer's voice, the one I use for meetings,' says Ms Hunt.

(www.makethemostofyourvoice.com/)†

Of course, the tendency to use a 'telephone voice', in which the regional features of the speaker's accent are minimised, is a well-known phenomenon. Howard Giles showed that speakers tend to **accommodate** their accent to that of their interlocutor, converging with, i.e.

---

*Presumably this should read 'from Worksop', which is not in South Yorkshire, but in Nottinghamshire.
† This extract, posted on the company's website, has been taken from the article which appears on p. 35 as Text 5: Accent Reduction.

becoming more similar to, the accent of somebody they like or wish to impress, and diverging from the accent of somebody they dislike. Most people will modify their accent when attending a job interview, just as they will modify their appearance, by wearing a smart suit, for example. Students who have moved away to a university in a different city often remark how their accent becomes 'broader' when they return home, or when they speak to family members on the telephone. The 'accent-reduction' programmes work on the assumption that a regional accent will always be perceived negatively in the workplace, and that some speakers need help to 'accommodate' their accent. However, there is also evidence that some regional accents evoke a positive response, and can be an asset in certain occupations. The recent rise of call centres in the UK has seen many of these centres located in regions of England with strong and recognisable local accents, or in Ireland, Scotland or Wales. In many cases, the opening of one of these call centres was accompanied by a report of research carried out into the perception of the local accent. Just as Giles's work predicted, customers felt more comfortable interacting with an operator with a 'friendly' regional accent. An article by Stephen Khan in the *Observer*, 24 August 2003, discusses customers' reactions to the newly-deregulated directory enquiries services in the UK:

> Bin the brogue and adopt a cut-glass Home Counties voice. That was once the best advice for ambitious Celts and Northerners, but now, amid the chaos of directory inquiry deregulation, comes victory for regional accents.
>
> Shrill, public school English is no match for a soft Scottish lilt, charming Irish chirp or warm Welsh warble when dealing with irate callers, and most inquiries to the controversial new 118 numbers are being handled by centres in northern England and the Celtic fringe. You may not be told the price of the call, you may not even get the right number, but at least you will be greeted by a dulcet tone.
>
> The dominance of soft regional accents in call centres may be put down to the establishment of operations in areas where land is cheaper and jobs harder to come by than in the South-East, but telecoms bosses admit that accents played a part in determining where they settled.
>
> British Telecom expects to lose up to 30 per cent of its business with the introduction of competition and the passing of its 192 number, but is banking on its 31 UK call centres to maintain a lead over more than a dozen newcomers. Only three of the BT call centres are in the South-East – at Croydon, Brentwood and Oxford – while BT's backbone is provided by cities such as Aberdeen,

Dundee, Newcastle and Cardiff. A BT spokesman agreed that 'regional accents do go down well'.

(accessed at http://observer.guardian.co.uk/ uk_news/story/0,,1028437,00.html)

The term 'soft regional accents' is not a precise linguistic description, but the accents used by call-centre operators are not the broadest regional accents, but what we might call **mild** accents, with the strongest and most stigmatised regional features modified or eliminated. Giles found that reactions to mild regional accents were consistently more positive than to broad ones: the call-centre workers avoid both the 'unfriendly' connotations of RP, and the 'uneducated' associations of broad regional accents, and so are acceptable to a wide range of callers.

Apart from the research conducted on behalf of call centres and that carried out by academics, more light-hearted surveys appear from time to time, dealing with the attractiveness or otherwise of various accents. One such survey appeared in the women's magazine *Bella* in 1999. Under the headline 'Which accents turn you on?' the report informed us that 1,000 men and women had been interviewed 'to rate which accents send temperatures soaring'. The accents concerned were all from the British Isles: the 'sexiest' was Scots, followed by Southern Irish and Welsh; the highest-rated English accent was Geordie in fourth place, while RP trailed in at sixth and Birmingham, as usual, was rated lowest. The author of the article does not tell us whether the 1,000 interviewees came from England or across the British Isles, but it does appear that 'non-English' accents were favoured most highly, perhaps because, as national, rather than regional, accents, they are no longer judged against RP. Certainly, the former dominance of the BBC by RP-accented newsreaders has given way to presenters with Scots, Welsh and Irish accents: when the BBC's 6 p.m. news broadcast was restyled in the 1990s, a focus group chose the Welsh newsreader, Huw Edwards, over an RP-accented female newsreader, on the basis that the latter sounded 'too snooty'. The favourite English accent of the *Bella* interviewees, Geordie, is very prominent on light entertainment programmes on British TV, but we have yet to hear a Geordie newsreader outside regional TV. Although RP is not as positively evaluated as it was when Strongman and Woosley, and Howard Giles conducted their surveys in the 1960s and 1970s, the hierarchy of accents appears to have changed very little since then, with the non-English accents perceived more favourably than the English regional ones, which in turn, are associated with social attractiveness rather than prestige, and poor old 'Brummie' at the bottom of the heap. For the most part, speakers evaluate their own accent in the same way as 'outsiders' do, at least within the same country: J.R. Edwards refers to 'the general tendency for non-standard speakers to accept the larger, and negative, stereotypes of their own speech' (1979: 87). One exception to this rule found in the *Bella* survey was that, while 10 per cent of their interviewees overall rated the Geordie accent the 'sexiest', the proportion of Tynesiders rating Geordie (i.e. their own accent) highest was 'almost a third'. This high degree of accent loyalty was not found elsewhere in England: Midlanders, along with the rest of those interviewed, regarded 'Brummie' as the 'worst' accent. This could be because Geordies have a very strong sense of regional identity.

The perception of RP as 'snooty' is not confined to Britain: in other English-speaking countries, especially the US, RP may be evaluated negatively because it carries connotations of colonialism, or positively, because it is associated with 'class'. It has been observed that many arch-villains in American films, from Scar in *The Lion King* to the Sheriff of Nottingham in *Robin Hood, Prince of Thieves* (in which Robin speaks with an American accent), are played by British actors with RP accents. The British villain, from Christopher Lee to Alan Rickman, has become a stereotype in itself, alongside the 'redneck' from the Southern states of the US and the broad-Australian-speaking 'larrikin'. Just as these stereotypes bear little or no relation to reality, so there is absolutely no correlation between RP-speaking and intelligence, or, for that matter, a Geordie accent and friendliness: you are quite likely to meet a stupid RP-speaker (note the alternative stereotype of the 'upper-class twit', such as Bertie Wooster or comedian Harry Enfield's character 'Tim Nice-but-Dim'), an educated, liberal Southerner in the US (Jimmy Carter springs to mind), or, indeed, an unfriendly Geordie.

Activity

In 1951, David Abercrombie wrote about what he termed the 'accent bar' that divided RP-speakers from those with regional accents in England. He concluded 'there is no doubt that RP is a privileged accent, your social life, or your career, or both, may be affected by whether you possess it or not' (1951: 10–15). Just 11 years later, A.C. Gimson wrote 'RP itself can be a handicap if used in inappropriate social situations, since it might be taken as a mark of affectation, or a desire to emphasize social superiority' (1962). Text 5: Accent Reduction is taken from an article by Colin Cottell in the *Guardian*, Saturday 20 December 2003. Read this, and then discuss the following questions in class.

1   Are there any accents that you dislike? If so, can you think of reasons why this is so?

2   Would you prefer to listen to the news read by an RP-speaker, or a presenter with a different national or regional accent?

3   Have you ever called, or been called by, a call centre in which the operator has an accent different from your own? What was your reaction?

4   Do you agree that a regional accent can be a disadvantage in certain jobs? If so, do you think this is because of 'accentism', which, like other '-isms' such as ageism and sexism, should be outlawed?

5   Can you think of successful people who have regional accents?

6   What do you think of 'accent-reduction' programmes? Would you ever consider taking one of these?

Text 5: Accent Reduction

SOME PEOPLE will do what ever it takes to get ahead in their career. Change job, move house, ingratiate themselves with the boss. Even change their accent.

'I want to neutralise my accent,' says Victoria Hardy an image consultant. She moved to Glasgow after a childhood spent in the North East. Now Ms Hardy is taking lessons from Derek Rogers, a language and accent specialist from Glasgow.

'I am doing it for career purposes really, to achieve maximum impact when I speak so everyone understands what I am saying,' she says.

You might think that Ms Hardy is paranoid or insecure. But a recent study by the Aziz Corporation, a firm of image consultants, suggests otherwise. It found that 46% of company directors believe that having a strong regional accent is considered a disadvantage to business success.

It also showed that some accents are more unequal than others. Liverpudlian, brummie, west country and cockney accents came out worst. But home counties and Scottish accents are seen as career assets.

The study confirmed previous research, which showed that having the wrong type of accent can affect your career. It also added credence to the belief that the 'acceptability' of local accents is a key factor in companies' decisions about where to locate.

'I think it is blind prejudice,' says Khalid Aziz, chairman of the Aziz Corporation. 'It seems to be pretty general. It is not just that southerners don't like people from the north; traditionally the Scots don't like the English. It works all ways round. The fact is that it is not what you say, but the way that you say it.'

Jenni Hunt, a lawyer from Wimbledon, and originally from Worksop used to speak with a south Yorkshire accent. But after leaving her home town 16 years ago, she says she ditched her twang. 'I wanted to be taken seriously and to take myself seriously. I am pretty sure that it has helped my career,' she says.

In an attempt to boost her other career performing voiceovers she is having one-to-one sessions with Frances Parkes, a speech coach, and head of www.make themostofyourvoice.com 'When I ring up agents I speak with my lawyers voice, the one I use for meetings,' says Ms Hunt.

People make assumptions about you based on your accent, says Ms Hardy. 'Every accent has a stigma attached to it in various ways. I don't want people to think about my accent. I want them to focus on what I am actually saying.'

Derek Rogers says: 'It is largely to do with the image that people have of the place that those people come from. People in the south of England tend generally to dislike Birmingham accents because they perceive Birmingham to be a large nasty town full of large nasty working class people.'

Steve Thorne, a lecturer in English language at the University of Birming-ham adds: 'Accent preference can affect a person's employability.' His thesis, 'Birmingham English – A Socio-linguistic Study', showed not only that linguistic preferences were widespread, but that people acted upon them.

Mr Aziz says: 'In jobs where high levels of communication are required, I think there are issues. It is unlikely that you would have someone in corporate bank-ing speaking with a regional British accent, but not impossible. I can't think of any [exceptions].'

'Certainly Scots are accepted. In fact, much of banking is dominated by Scots, so that is not the problem it was, but I don't know of any Scousers at the top of corporate banking.'

'Once you get over the early stages of meeting someone, that is a different situ-ation and people overcome their initial prejudice, but you might not get a second chance to make an initial impression.'

It is that old thing about the first impressions being the most important when meeting someone, says Steve Pearse, a policy specialist at the Liverpool Chamber of Commerce.

He echoes the findings of Albert Mehrabian, a social psychologist, who discovered that 38% of a first impression is based on the way we sound, compared to just 7% on what we say.

Accent is also a problem for some of Britain's ethnic communities, says Ms Parkes.

Take people from Northern India, for example: 'When they say winner they will be pronouncing it vinner.' This is 'very upsetting' for them, she says. 'They are conscious of being outside the ballpark because the way they speak is saying "I belong to a different tribe".'

Mr Pearse says: 'It is a question of degree. If an accent is too pronounced you have got a problem. And people won't understand you.'

But contrary to the general perception of Scouse, a number of businesses perceive it as 'friendly', persuading companies such as United Airlines and TV shopping channel QVC to set up contact centres in the area.

Even so, Mr Pearse admits that outside show business 'it is difficult to think of too many people with a pronounced accent who have been successful.'

To get to the top 'you may have to moderate your own voice to a certain degree,' he says regretfully.

The situation has changed over the past 10 years 'with all the multinational people now living with us in the UK', and 'the class system going down the shoot,' says Ms Parkes. The preference for a clear upper English class accent is largely confined to barristers at a 'few inns of court,' she says.

Does that hold for the top jobs in business? Mr Aziz doesn't agree. 'One would like to believe it, but we are not seeing it yet,' he says.

'Greg Dyke has risen to the top of the world's foremost communications organisation, and he certainly does not speak with an RP accent – but the chairman that appointed him, Christopher Bland, certainly does.'

The issue of accents is not being taken seriously enough says Mr Thorne. 'People seem to look on discrimination based on how people use language as a minor form of prejudice in comparison to racism, or ageism, or sexism, but I don't think it is any less serious at all.'

There are quite a few linguists who favour legislation along the lines of banning discrimination against what they call accentism. However, it not something that employers appear to take seriously.

An HSBC spokesperson said that the bank didn't have a policy on accents. She said: 'We don't record details of the accents of people we appoint.' Continues Mr Thorne: 'In 2001 there was the case of a Chinese woman who could speak English very well but obviously had a Chinese accent and she was sacked because of that. She took it to court and it found in her favour.'

There are laws in other countries, which forbid it too, he says.

So what about elocution lessons? 'Absolutely unnecessary,' says Mr Thorne. We are beginning to see people slipping through the net of prejudice, he says pointing to professor Carl Chinn, a Birmingham historian, radio broadcaster, and author, who has 'a really thick Brummie accent,' and is beginning to be recognised outside the region.

'You don't have to get rid of you accent to get on in life,' he concludes.

Ms Hardy is not deterred, however. 'Eventually in a year, I will look back and think, yeh, I do speak a bit differently now.' But whether it makes much difference to her career remains to be seen. ■

(The *Guardian* Jobs and Money, 20 December 2003, accessed at www.guardian. co.uk/guardian_jobs_and_money/story/0,,1110356,00.html#article_continue)

(There is no commentary for this activity.)

Activity

Text 6: The North Wind and the Sun is the fable of the North Wind and the Sun, which has often been used as a reading passage in linguistic experiments. If you have a friend or classmate who is 'good at accents', you could ask him or her to read the passage in a number of different accents, otherwise you should ask people of roughly the same age and the same gender but with different accents to read it. Include somebody with a fairly broad local accent, somebody with an accent nearer to RP (or whatever the prestige accent is in your country, if you are outside the UK), and as many other regional accents as you can find. Record the readings, using any medium that is easy to carry and provides good quality recordings. Then ask friends, relatives, or whoever is willing, to listen to the recordings and answer the questionnaire below, under the assumption that they are hearing different speakers. If you have access to the appropriate technology and expertise, you might record these digitally, put the sound files on a website and devise a web-based questionnaire. Obviously, you should avoid asking people to fill out the questionnaire if they know and would recognise any of the speakers.

The questionnaire includes the kind of questions asked in experiments carried out by Giles, Lambert and Labov. Questions 1 and 6 identify how prestigious speakers or accents are considered, while questions 2–5 measure the social attractiveness of speakers or accents. Typically, listeners judge RP or other prestige varieties high on the 'prestige' scales, but low on the 'social attractiveness' scales. Some people will feel uncomfortable about answering these questions, as they will recognise that it's unfair to judge people on their voice alone. Yet we all make such judgements and have 'gut reactions' to speakers every day. When I tried this experiment with a class of university students, all of whom were studying linguistics, the results were very consistent. Even though all the speakers whose voices they heard were well educated and in white-collar jobs, they judged those with regional accents to be uneducated and in low-prestige jobs, with only the speaker with a near-RP accent judged as intelligent. Conversely, all the speakers with (Northern) regional accents were judged as friendly and honest.

Text 6: The North Wind and the Sun

The North Wind and the Sun were disputing which of them was stronger, when a traveller came along wrapped in a warm cloak. They agreed that the one who first succeeded in making the traveller take off his cloak should be considered stronger than the other. Then the North Wind blew as hard as he could, but the more he blew, the more closely did the traveller fold his cloak around him; and at last the North Wind gave up the attempt. Then the Sun shone out warmly, and immediately the traveller took off his cloak. And so the North Wind was obliged to confess that the Sun was the stronger of the two.

Questionnaire

Thank you for agreeing to take part in our project. We are interested in reactions to people's voices, such as when heard on the 'phone. You will hear a number of voices reading the same passage. On the basis of your reaction to the voice alone, please answer the following questions. Where there is a scale, 1 is low (e.g. 'least intelligent', 9 is high, e.g. 'most intelligent'.

1 How intelligent do you think this speaker is? (Please circle the appropriate number.)

    1   2   3   4   5   6   7   8   9

2 How friendly do you think this speaker is? (Please circle the appropriate number.)

    1   2   3   4   5   6   7   8   9

3 How honest do you think this speaker is? (Please circle the appropriate number.)

    1   2   3   4   5   6   7   8   9

4 How trustworthy do you think this speaker is? (Please circle the appropriate number.)

    1   2   3   4   5   6   7   8   9

5 How attractive do you think this speaker is? (Please circle the appropriate number.)

    1   2   3   4   5   6   7   8   9

6 What kind of a job do you think this speaker does, or would do in the future?

(There is no commentary for this activity.)

SUMMARY

In this unit, we have discussed research into stereotyped reactions to accents and the ways in which various accents of English, both regional and national, are perceived. Although there is no factual evidence that speaking with a regional accent is associated with any trait of personality, research by social psychologists such as Howard Giles and sociolinguists such as William Labov does demonstrate that people in a particular speech community hold very strong and consistent stereotypes of speakers with certain accents. Typically, rural accents are judged to be more pleasant than urban ones, and speakers of the prestige accent (RP in England) are judged to be more intelligent, but less friendly than speakers of regional accents. These stereotyped reactions can affect customers' reactions to telesales operators, so call centres are often placed in regions where the accent is judged to be 'friendly'. Awareness of these reactions has led to the introduction of 'accent-reduction' programmes for people who believe that their accents will lead to them being perceived as less intelligent or competent than they would like, and so may harm their job prospects.

Extension

Collect a number of newspaper articles about attitudes to accents, either from current issues, or from the online archives listed under the heading Web-based resources (p. 107). These may be about 'accent-reduction' programmes, like that shown in Text 5: Accent Reduction, or may discuss the siting of call centres, or may simply be about accents. Is there a consistent pattern of positive or negative attitudes to particular accents? What issues arise from the siting of call centres overseas in countries such as India, where English is used as a second language?

Recognising accents

We saw in Unit three that listeners have very strong reactions to regional accents, based on stereotypes of speakers from certain regions being more friendly, or of RP-speakers as being intelligent. Of course, these stereotypes have no basis in reality: speaking with an RP accent does not make somebody more intelligent, nor does speaking with a Geordie accent make them more friendly.

Although individuals find certain accents more attractive, this usually has little to do with the pleasantness of the sound. When recordings of English accents are played to speakers of other languages, the accents judged as 'harsh' or 'nasal' by native speakers are perceived as being as pleasant as any other. Individual features of accents can be judged as prestigious in one place and stigmatised in another. An example of this is the pronunciation of words like CAR, FARM with the <r> appearing at the end of a word, or before another consonant, pronounced as /r/. In England, such pronunciations are only heard in the South West, or in parts of Lancashire, and speakers who pronounce the /r/ are judged to be either 'country bumpkins' or comic Northerners. In the US, on the other hand, it is the accents with /r/, known as **rhotic** accents, that are considered prestigious, or even 'normal': /r/-less or non-rhotic accents are those of the South, or of African-Americans, or of working-class New Yorkers, all groups of speakers who have been negatively stereotyped. In England, pronunciations with /r/ are becoming rarer, while in the US, they are becoming more common. This proves that there is nothing inherently clever or prestigious about pronouncing or not pronouncing the <r>: accents are judged as prestigious or not according to what is judged to be the social profile of their speakers, and as 'attractive' or not according to stereotypical views of the people and places with which they are associated, not the inherent beauty of their sound.

It is important to bear this in mind when we discuss recent changes that have been viewed as 'lazy', such as the glottalisation of /t/ in, for example, HAT, BUTTER. Many people think that this involves 'dropping' the /t/, whereas in fact the 'new' pronunciation has a glottal stop /ʔ/, which is just a different consonant. Even where a 'letter' has been 'dropped', what is viewed as lazy by one generation is accepted as normal by the next: the /r/-less pronunciation of words such as CAR, FARM, was first noticed in England in the late eighteenth century, but it was then seen as an incorrect 'Cockney' pronunciation. It was still being condemned well into the nineteenth century, but is now 'normal' in RP and many other English accents. By the end of this century, if not sooner, the same may well be said of glottal stops.

In Unit three, we discussed the ways in which we react to speakers of certain accents according to stereotypes associated with those accents. In order to do this, we must be able to recognise regional accents, at least to some extent. We all know people who say 'I'm hopeless at accents' because they feel unable to differentiate between, for instance, a Lancashire and a Yorkshire accent, but even these people will react to speakers of those accents according to their view of 'Northerners'. A story in the Bible demonstrates that, since ancient times, people have been able to recognise different accents, sometimes with deadly consequences.

> And the Gileadites seized the passages of the Jordan before the Ephraimites; and it was so, that when those Ephraimites who had escaped said, 'Let me go over,' that the men of Gilead said unto him, 'Art thou an Ephraimite?' If he said, 'Nay,' then said they unto him, 'Say now "Shibboleth."' And he said 'Sibboleth,' for he could not frame to pronounce it right. Then they took him and slew him at the passages of the Jordan; and there fell at that time of the Ephraimites forty and two thousand.
>
> (Judges 12: 5–6, King James version of the Bible)

Here, the Gileadites knew that the difference between their accent and that of the Ephraimites was that the latter could not pronounce <sh> as /ʃ/ but said /s/ instead. An easy way to detect the enemy, then, was to ask them to say the Hebrew word *shibboleth*.

This story has given us the word 'shibboleth', defined by the *OED* as follows:

1   A word or sound which a person is unable to pronounce correctly; a word used as a test for detecting foreigners, or persons from another district, by their pronunciation.

2   A peculiarity of pronunciation or accent indicative of a person's origin.

In the case of the Ephraimites, recognition of an accent was a matter of life and death, but stories of modern-day 'shibboleths' are not unusual. It is said that border guards in the US detect Canadians by asking them to recite the alphabet: the last letter is pronounced /zed/ by Canadians, but /ziː/ by citizens of the US. The tendency to end sentences with *eh?* is likewise cited as a useful shibboleth by which Canadians can be identified. Shibboleths can also be the subject of jokes or friendly banter between rival groups: the phrase *fish and chips* acts as a shibboleth both for Australians and New Zealanders: the former pronounce it with what sounds like a long /iː/ vowel, which is perceived as '*feesh and cheeps*', while the 'Kiwi' pronunciation with a vowel like **schwa** (the vowel heard in unstressed syllables at the end of words like BETTER), sounds to Australians like '*fush and chups*'. This would be a very good test for distinguishing Australian accents from New Zealand ones, were it not for the fact that English-speaking South Africans also say '*fush and chups*'. In some cases, shibboleths are only known by groups of speakers who live very close to each other: the cities of Newcastle-upon-Tyne and Sunderland in the North East of England are only ten miles apart, but there is a very strong rivalry between citizens of these two places, especially in the context of football. When Newcastle United play against Sunderland, the Newcastle fans jangle keys in the air and shout 'whaes keys are these keys?'. This would be baffling to strangers, but the point being made is that people from Sunderland ('Mackems') pronounce the words *whaes* ('whose'), *these* and *keys* with a **diphthong** /ei/, while those from Newcastle ('Geordies') use a **monophthong** /iː/. Even the nickname for Sunderlanders, 'Mackem', derives from a local shibboleth: in the days of shipbuilding, workers in Sunderland would /mak/ (*make*) the ships and /tak/ (*take*) them up the River Wear. The pronunciation with short /a/ was, and still is, characteristic of Sunderland. People from other parts of the UK have great difficulty telling North Eastern accents apart, tending to perceive them all as 'Geordie', but local differences are well recognised within the North East.

Incidentally, not all shibboleths are features of accent: sometimes a word or a grammatical construction is so well known as characteristic of a certain place that it becomes a shibboleth. A good example of this was used in an episode of *Law and Order: Criminal Intent* in which the detective identified a murder suspect as coming from Western Pennsylvania because she used the phrase '*redd up*' meaning to tidy a room. The 'Pittsburghese' T-shirt illustrated in Unit two (Text 4, p. 27) includes this among a list of words and phrases typical of the speech of this city in Western Pennsylvania.

Activity

Consider the following questions and if possible discuss them in groups:

1   Are there any shibboleths in your region that distinguish speakers from one city, town or village, from another? Make a list of these.

2   Does your local team (whatever sport is important in your locality) have a close rival, and, if so, are features of the 'rival' accent picked out as shibboleths?

3   Are you aware of any other shibboleths or stories of these, from whatever region?

(There is no commentary for this activity.)

As we have seen in the previous section, shibboleths are features of speech that are so well known, at least within their locality, that they can be used to identify differences between speakers who otherwise might sound alike. When it comes to recognising differences between accents from further afield, it is often the case that we recognise broader distinctions such as 'Northern' versus 'Southern' accents, but that the ability to tell accents apart depends on experience. Exposure of accents on TV and radio often leads to them being easier to identify. For instance, over the last five to ten years, a number of celebrities from Bolton, Lancashire have had a great deal of exposure in the British media, such as comedians Victoria Wood and Peter Kay, and DJs/presenters Sarah Cox and Vernon Kay. This has led to the broad and traditional Bolton accent (quite different from that of nearby metropolitan Manchester) becoming recognised. A TV advertisement for Knorr sauces has Vernon Kay speaking the voiceover with the catchphrase: 'just say Knorr to boring food'. The pun in this catchphrase only makes sense if viewers recognise that, in the Bolton accent *no* has the same vowel /ɔː/ as *Knorr*.

As linguists, we need to be able to recognise the major differences between accents of English without having to rely on encountering these in person or in the media. Peter Trudgill (1999: 68) suggests that it is possible to differentiate all the major regional accents of England by using the sentence 'very few cars made it up the long hill' such that no two speakers from different regions will pronounce all of these words in the same way. This provides us with a good starting point, but we will also look at other features that differentiate accents within Trudgill's broader regions. Let us first take Trudgill's sentence word by word.

'Very'

The key feature here is the final vowel of words such as *very, happy, Gary*, etc. This can be pronounced either as /i/ or even /iː/ (as in MEET); or as /ɪ/ (as in HIT), or even as /ɛ/ (as in LET). The pronunciations with /i(ː)/ is found in RP, in the whole of the South of England and much of the Midlands, as well as Wales, but it is also found in some Northern accents, i.e. those of Merseyside, Humberside and the North East. The areas in which /ɪ/ or /ɛ/ are used are those which make up the rest of the North of England: most of Lancashire, Cumbria and Yorkshire. Within the North, this feature differentiates Manchester from Liverpool, Teesside from neighbouring North Yorkshire, and Hull from the rest of Yorkshire. There is evidence that the /iː/ pronunciation is spreading into areas in which it was formerly not heard, such as Sheffield and Derby, both in what would generally be viewed as the border between the North and the Midlands, so this may not be such a good diagnostic in future.

'Few'

In most English accents, words like *few, duty, human* have the vowel spelt <ew> or <u> pronounced as /juː/ (as in YOU). However, a pronunciation without the /j/ is characteristic of East Anglia and the bordering areas of the East Midlands, and what Hughes, Trudgill and Watt (2005) term the 'South Midlands', i.e. Bedfordshire and Northamptonshire. Here, the pronunciation is /fuː/ as in the first syllable of FOOL. This is a well-known feature of East Anglian accents, popularised in the Bernard Matthews turkey advertisements on TV ('They're bootiful'), but this pronunciation is more widespread when used with a restricted set of words in which the vowel follows /d/, /t/ or /n/, such as *due*, *tune*, *news*. These words have /uː/ rather than /juː/ in American English, and in some Southern accents of England, notably that of London. So, the loss of /j/ in words such as *few*, *beautiful* and *human* is characteristic of Eastern accents in England, especially East Anglian, but the same pronunciation in *news* and, to a lesser extent *due*, *tune* is less diagnostic.

'Cars'

Trudgill includes the word CARS in his sentence because it includes <r> before a consonant. We have already seen that accents in which the /r/ is pronounced (rhotic accents) are rare in England, confined to the South West and parts of Central Lancashire, and that even in these areas the /r/ is less likely to be pronounced by younger people. This is an example of a recessive or relict feature, one that was formerly more widespread but is now confined to what, from a metropolitan point of view, night be termed 'peripheral' areas. Even in Scotland, where the pronunciation of /r/ has been seen as a national feature, there is evidence that younger speakers in the two largest cities, Glasgow and Edinburgh, are beginning to pronounce words such as CAR without it. So, an accent that otherwise sounds Northern but has /r/ in CARS is probably from Central Lancashire, but a younger person from this area might well pronounce CARS without /r/, so this is not a foolproof diagnostic. Irish accents tend to be rhotic, as do those of Canada, while in the US non-rhotic accents are becoming rarer, but are found in the South, in the speech of African-Americans and in a few Eastern cities such as Boston. Otherwise, most varieties of English, such as Australian and New Zealand English, tend to be non-rhotic.

'Made'

This word includes a vowel that is pronounced as a diphthong /ei/ in RP but as a monopthong /eː/ in some accents. According to Hughes, Trudgill and Watt (2005), pronunciations with /ei/ are found throughout most of the South and East of England and in the Midlands. In the North, the only area in which this diphthong is found is Merseyside, and it is not found in Wales, Scotland or Ireland. In the South West, they cite this feature as the only one differentiating the eastern South West (with /ei/) from the western South West. Although Hughes, Trudgill and Watt state that those regions without the diphthongal pronunciation have a monophthong /eː/, this is over-simplified. In the North East, the traditional pronunciation of Tyneside has a different diphthong /iə/, and some areas of the North may have pronunciations more like /ɛː/ (as in HAIR). However, it is certainly true that the /ei/ diphthong differentiates the Liverpool accent from the more traditional accents of neighbouring areas of Lancashire.

'Up'

This word contains the vowel that is one of the most diagnostic features of 'Northern' versus 'Southern' accents in England. In the whole of the North and most of the Midlands, this word has the same vowel as that in FOOT, i.e. /ʊ/ but in the South a distinct vowel /ʌ/ is used. What is important here is not so much the exact pronunciation of the vowel, since educated or 'posh' Northerners may well pronounce UP with a vowel more like that at the end of e.g. BETTER, but whether pairs of words such as PUSS ('cat') and PUS ('matter'); COULD ('was able to'); and CUD ('what cows chew'); PUT ('to place') and PUTT (as in golf) sound identical. For Northerners, there is no difference between the words in these pairs, but for Southerners there clearly is, with /ʊ/ in the first of each pair and /ʌ/ in the second. Along with the vowel in words like BATH (not included in Trudgill's sentence, but discussed later) this is one of the best-known features marking the 'North–South divide' in accents of England. Accents of Scotland, Ireland and Wales, and those outside the UK, all distinguish between the words in these pairs, though some of these accents, notably those of South Wales, use a vowel much more like schwa in words such as PUS, CUD and PUTT.

'Long'

The diagnostic feature here is the pronunciation of <ng> at the end of the word. In most accents of English, this sequence of consonants in spelling is pronounced as a single **velar nasal** consonant /ŋ/. However, in accents of Central Lancashire, Merseyside, the North West Midlands and the West Midlands, the <g> is pronounced as well, so we have a sequence /ŋg/. These areas as defined by Hughes, Trudgill and Watt actually make up one continuous area covering the West of England from about Coventry to Preston and including Manchester and even Sheffield. Speakers from these areas tend not to realise that their pronunciation of words such as LONG is in any way 'different', because, throughout (and beyond) the UK, more attention is paid to the pronunciation of final

<ing> in words such as WALKING. The pronunciation with /n/ rather than /ŋ/ is highly stigmatised, and characteristic of the speech of less educated and/or lower-class persons in every region. The exception to this is the accent of older, very upper-class English speakers, who are stereotypically fond of *huntin', shootin' and fishin'*. In the detective novels of Dorothy M. Sayers, set in the 1920s and 1930s, the aristocratic hero, Lord Peter Wimsey, affects this pronunciation when he wishes to pose as an 'upper class twit' in order to disarm the villain. Unusually, the /ɪn/ pronunciation is a shibboleth of both upper- and lower-class speech in the UK. This pronunciation is often quite wrongly termed 'dropping the g': as we have seen, the only people who actually pronounce a /g/ in these words are those who have /ŋg/ in LONG. For speakers in these areas, pronunciations such as /sɪtɪŋg/ are the 'posh' equivalents of, for example, /sɪtɪn/. Because these speakers are quite unselfconscious about their pronunciation of words such as LONG, this is a good diagnostic of these accents.

'Hill'

In this word, our attention is on two features: the pronunciation or otherwise of the initial <h>, and the final /l/. Along with the /ɪn/ pronunciation of, for example, SITTING discussed earlier, 'h-dropping' (a more accurate term in this case) is one of the strongest shibboleths of lower-class and/or uneducated speech in England. However, not all English accents involve 'h-dropping' to the same degree. The table below shows results from surveys conducted by Petyt (1985) in West Yorkshire, and by Trudgill (1974) in Norwich. In each case, the higher the score, the greater the proportion of 'h-dropping' in the speech of that group.

Petyt (1977)		Trudgill (1974)	
Upper middle class	12	Upper middle class	6
Lower middle class	28	Lower middle class	14
Upper working class	67	Upper working class	40
Middle working class	89	Middle working class	60
Lower working class	93	Lower working class	60

(after Chambers and Trudgill 1998: 59)

What is apparent here is that in both areas, the proportion of 'h-dropping' increases as we go lower down the social scale, but that for every social group, 'h-dropping' is more common in West Yorkshire than it is in Norwich. This is because East Anglia is one of the few regions of England in which initial <h> is pronounced /h/ in the traditional dialect. In Norwich, the largest town in the region, the accent seems to have been influenced more recently by the pronunciation of other areas, probably London. Because 'h-dropping' is so common, we tend to refer to 'h-retaining' accents, as these are in the minority, at least in England. The only areas of England in which 'h' is retained are, according to Hughes, Trudgill and Watt, East Anglia and the North East. It is certainly the case that 'h-dropping' is very rare in Newcastle, except when the <h> occurs in a word that is very frequently used and is unstressed, such as 'I saw (h)im'; but Tynesiders believe that 'h-dropping' is much more common in Sunderland, only 10 miles south. Some years ago, I took part in a phone-in programme on Radio Newcastle where the subject for discussion was, of course, local dialect. One caller informed me that people from Sunderland 'couldn't pronounce their aitches' and that her daughter, having moved from Newcastle to Washington (now included in the City of Sunderland) was the only one in her class who could pronounce her aitches properly. Within the North East, 'h-dropping' is a shibboleth of regional rather than social speech, as even the most working-class Geordie will shout 'Howay the lads!' in support of his football team.

The final /l/ of *hill* is pronounced as a **dark** [ɫ] in RP and many other English accents. The dark [ɫ] is more vowel-like than the **clear** [l]: when pronouncing the former, the tongue does not touch the top of the mouth, while for a clear [l] as in *hilly* it does. This is usually described as an **allophonic** distinction in English, as the occurrence of [ɫ] or [l] can be predicted from the environment: [ɫ] after vowels, [l] before or between vowels. Some accents do not have this distinction: in Tyneside and Welsh English, the /l/ is always clear, so *hill, hilly* would both have [l]. On the other hand, some Southern accents **vocalise** the /l/ further, so that it becomes either [ʊɫ] or even [ɪʊ]. This extreme vocalisation is a feature of London and Estuary English.

Of course, there are other features which identify regional accents, but Trudgill devised this sentence in order to distinguish the major regional accents of England from each other, using the smallest number of diagnostic features. The pronunciation of words such as BATH is, if anything, a better diagnostic of 'Northern' (meaning Northern or Midland) accents than UP, because the short, 'Northern' pronunciation tends to be retained even by well-educated, upwardly-mobile Northerners. As Wells (1982: 354) states,

> there are many educated northerners who would not be caught dead doing something so vulgar as to pronounce STRUT words with /ʌ/, but who would feel it a denial of their identity as northerners to say BATH words with anything other than short [a].

(Note, here Wells used square brackets [ ] to identify a more subtle **phonetic** distinction between variant pronunciations.)

Other features may be more salient than those in Trudgill's test sentence, but may only identify very specific local accents rather than those used over a wider region, or they may provide extra clues to an accent that could already be identified using Trudgill's sentence alone. For instance, the accent of Hull is often identified by the pronunciation of the vowel in words such as NURSE, which is pronounced /ɛː/ as in FAIR. A pun on this pronunciation is found in the nickname of one of the city's rugby teams, Hull FC, who are known as the Airlie Birds. However, the accent of Hull could be identified using Trudgill's sentence alone, since Humberside is the only region in which MADE would have a monophthong, but VERY would have the [iː] pronunciation.

Activity

1   In pairs, take turns to say the sentence 'Very few cars made it up the long hill'. The person not speaking should listen to the way in which each of the words discussed above is pronounced and take notes. Then, using the information provided for each of the words, see whether you can identify the regional accent using this information alone.

2   It may be the case that every body in your class has the same accent, because they have all lived in the same area for all or most of their lives. If this is the case, the teacher should read the sentence out to the whole class, who should then try to identify his or her regional accent.

3   Discuss your findings in class. Are there other features of the accents concerned which, in your view, are more important as diagnostics? Are these the same as the 'shibboleths' discussed earlier?

Commentary

This commentary is based on my own reading of the sentence.

Very   I pronounce this with /iː/, so this rules out most of Lancashire and Yorkshire, except for the area close to Liverpool.

Few   I pronounce this as /fjuː/, so this rules out the eastern areas of East Anglia, the East Midlands, Northamptonshire and Bedfordshire.

Cars   I do not pronounce the /r/ in this word, so this rules out the South West, Central Lancashire, Scotland and Ireland.

Made   I pronounce this with a diphthong /ei/, so this rules out everywhere in the North except Merseyside, and also rules out the western South West.

Up   I pronounce this with /ʊ/, so this rules out anywhere south of about Birmingham

Long   I pronounce this with final /ŋg/, indicating Central Lancashire, the North West Midlands, the West Midlands or Merseyside.

Hill   I pronounce the /h/ in this, indicating either the North East or East Anglia, or membership of a higher social class. I pronounce the /l/ as dark, but not vocalised, which rules out the North East and Wales on the one hand and London/Estuary on the other.

Putting all these clues together, all the evidence except the /h/ in HILL, points to either Merseyside or the North West or West Midlands. UP indicates North or Midlands, but CARS rules out Central Lancashire. VERY rules out most of Lancashire and Yorkshire; MADE rules out the North East, as well as most of Lancashire and Yorkshire; FEW rules out the East Midlands; and LONG points to Merseyside or the West or North West Midlands. HILL cannot be used to determine region, since the only two /h/-retaining areas, the North East and East Anglia, have already been ruled out, so here it must indicate social class and/or education.

I was born and spent the first 18 years of my life in Warrington, which is about 20 miles east of Liverpool, so the clues in Trudgill's sentence do pinpoint my regional accent quite accurately as Merseyside/North West Midlands. I would have dropped my aitches much more frequently when I was younger, but now pronounce them most of the time. This could either be due to social mobility and education, or to the fact that I spent the next 30 years of my life in Newcastle, an /h/-retaining city.

However, the clues in Trudgill's sentence did not rule out the possibility of my accent being West Midland, yet I have never been identified as a 'Brummie' by anybody who has heard me speak. Each regional accent has features that distinguish it from its neighbours: for instance, the West Midlands accent would pronounce MADE with a diphthong more like /ai/ in LIKE (which, in turn, would be pronounced /loik/), and the vowel in IT would be more like /i/ in SEE, as opposed to /ɪ/ in Merseyside. Trudgill's sentence is intended to provide clues that will distinguish the major regional accents of England using the smallest number of diagnostic features and, as such, it is very useful.

SUMMARY

In this unit, we have discussed the features that differentiate regional accents of English from each other. First, we have looked at the notion of shibboleths and salient features, which people within a speech community recognise as identifying a certain accent. We have then looked at the main features that differentiate accents of British English, as set out by Trudgill using the sentence 'Very few cars made it up the long hill.' Finally, we have discussed the fact that, while the features in this sentence can be used to differentiate the major regional varieties found in England, within a smaller geographical area other features often differentiate one accent from another.

Extension

Make a recording of yourself or a friend or family member from the same place reading the fable shown in Text 6: The North Wind and the Sun in Unit three (p. 39). Listen to it carefully (you will need to do this several times) and make a note of any features of pronunciation that you consider typical of your region. (You will find a list of phonetic symbols and descriptions of the sounds that they represent on pp. 103–104.) What features distinguish the accent of your region, town or city from those of other areas? Are these covered by the 'Very few cars made it up the long hill' sentence or not? If possible, when you have done this with your own recording, compare notes with somebody else who has carried out the same exercise.

Words and things

So far, we have concentrated on regional accents of English, and attitudes to these. However, regional **dialects** differ from each other both in terms of the words used (**lexis**) and the ways in which words are put together to form sentences (grammar). We will discuss dialect grammar in Unit six, but in this unit we will concentrate on lexis.

It is often said, both by linguists and non-linguists, that dialects are disappearing and, more particularly, that vocabulary is becoming more uniform throughout the UK, or even the English-speaking world. To a certain extent, this is true, as improved communications and global media allow new words and new meanings of words to spread very rapidly. For instance, just when older people had got used to the idea that *gay* meant 'homosexual' rather than 'happy', young people throughout the English-speaking world began using the word to mean 'uncool' ('That is *so* gay!'). This use of the word is associated with an age group rather than a region or even country, so could be classed as teenage slang. A recent example of a word coming to prominence in one region, then spreading over the whole country is *chav*, a term with similar connotations to the US 'white trash' and referring to a type of lower-class urban youth. This term seems to have originated in the South East of England, but is almost certainly derived from Romany (the language of travellers), where it simply means a boy or a child. Many British regional dialects have their own words for these people: in the North East, they are *charvers* (a term likewise taken from Romany); in

Glasgow they are *neds*; in Edinburgh *schemies* (from 'housing schemes'); in Liverpool *scallies*, but, at the time of writing, *chav* is being used all over the UK alongside or instead of the local terms. Of course the media, and especially websites, are largely responsible for drawing attention to, and therefore spreading, this new word.

On the other hand, some regional words do persist and are part of our everyday vocabulary. Take the word for a bread roll, such as you might buy from a sandwich shop at lunchtime. In Sheffield, this would be a *bread cake*, while a few miles south in Derbyshire, it would be a *cob*. In Manchester it would be a *barm cake* (*barm* is an old word for yeast) and elsewhere it might be a *bap*. In Newcastle, the sandwich shop would supply *stotty cakes*, though these are a type of large, flat, round loaf usually cut into quarters for sandwiches. One reason why such local differences persist may be that, even in the days of supermarkets, bread is still baked locally, so that local traditions and types survive. Thus the survival of a local word depends to some extent on there being a local thing to which it refers.

Of course, many of the traditional customs and practices for which dialect words provided labels have now disappeared. The *Survey of English Dialects* (*SED*) was begun just after the Second World War, because its founders, Harold Orton and Eugen Dieth, feared that universal access to radio (and therefore RP/Standard English), would lead to the loss of traditional dialect. In fact, many of the concepts for which they sought dialect words refer to very specific agricultural tools and practices, most of which have since disappeared as a result of the mechanisation of farming. For instance, speakers who have no use for a hay fork have no need for a dialectal term for such an implement, yet the *SED* found 86 different words for just such a tool, including *bedding-fork, cobbing-fork, forking-off-fork, hay-pikel, nine-mealer, pitch-fork, sheppeck* and *two-spean spud* (Upton *et al.* 1994: 197).

Although industry brought its own dialects (e.g. the language of coal miners, known as 'Pitmatic', in the North East), in the late twentieth century these too declined. Terms originally used in industries such as mining do persist for a while, but may well disappear in turn. Words for a meal taken to work varied from one coalfield to another: *bait* in the Northumberland and Durham coalfields, *snap* in Yorkshire, and *lunch* in Lancashire are all still used to some extent by all occupations in those areas to mean 'packed lunch', but they are much less common among the younger generation. Likewise, the steel industry had its own terminology that may no longer be known by younger speakers in steel-producing areas such as Sheffield: specific jobs such as *puddler* (a worker who 'puddles', or stirs molten iron) have disappeared, and the words have disappeared with them.

Dialect words concerned with traditional games have been lost along with these games, as children are no longer encouraged to play in the street, health and safety legislation outlaws them from the school playground, and toys and games become universal. Iona and Peter Opie produced their famous book *The Lore and Language of Schoolchildren* in 1959 to record games and terms that they felt might disappear. Terms for a 'truce' or 'time-out' were different in different areas: *skinchies* was used in the North East, *barleys* in the North West, *fainites* in the South East, etc. When asked whether they have a word for this concept, children today are either baffled, or simply suggest 'time-out', a term from American sports. If you ask older people what games they played as children, they will recall many with names that are local: people interviewed for the *Tyneside Linguistic Survey* (collected in Gateshead in 1969) mentioned games called *hitchie-dabbers*, *knocky-nine-door*, *multikitty* and *relievo*. One popular game found throughout the UK was marbles, played with coloured glass balls. Although the game was widespread, words for individual types of marble were dialectal: in the North East, terms such as *allies*, *liggers* and *penkers* were used for these.

However, the loss of dialect words is not always caused by the disappearance of the things or customs to which the words referred. The *SED* records widespread variation in words for everyday concepts. For instance, they found 33 different words for *throw*: *aim, check, chuck, clod, clot, cob, cobble, cop, fling, hain, hang, heave, hocks, holl, hoy, hull, jerk, peg, pelt, pitch, scop, shoot, shy, slew, sling, sock, stone, swail, throw, toss, whang, yack* and *yark*. (See the map in Upton and Widdowson (1996: 178). Upton and Widdowson say that there are 34 words, but they have counted *hoy* twice.) In such cases, the loss of local dialect words must be due to education (for many years, schools discouraged the use of dialect words) and/or improved communications, leading to a 'levelling out' of dialect terms.

This loss of distinct dialect terms is known as **lexical attrition**. A number of studies have attempted to measure the extent to which younger people still know or use traditional dialect words from their region, as recorded in the *SED* and/or dialect dictionaries. The words known and recognised make up the **passive vocabulary**, while those actually used make up the **active vocabulary**. Lourdes Burbano-Elizondo (2001) investigated both the active and passive vocabulary of high-school students in Newcastle and Sunderland. The questionnaire was designed to be 'user-friendly', providing multiple-choice answers for some words, for example:

> Let's see if you know these dialect words!
>
> 1. What is a *gowk?*
>
>   a. A hamster
>
>   b. A cuckoo
>
>   c. A pigeon
>
>   d. ???
>
> The d. option is 'don't know'. The 'correct' answer, which would indicate that the dialect word is part of the student's passive vocabulary, is b.

At the end of the questionnaire, the students were invited to provide a list of 'any other words that you, your friends or people in your family use that are characteristic of the speech of the area'.

Burbano-Elizondo found that:

◎ Girls knew more dialect words than boys.

◎ Even though the age gap was only three years (ages 13 to 16), older students knew more dialect words than younger students.

◎ Some traditional words were being retained, notably *lug* ('ear'), *gob* ('mouth'), *tattie* ('potato'), *hoy* ('throw'), *gadgie* ('old bloke'), *chuck* ('throw'), *bairn* ('child'), *netty* ('toilet').

◎ Others had been lost, namely *gowk* ('cuckoo' or 'April Fool'), *cuddy* ('donkey' or 'gypsy's horse'), *paddock* ('toad'), *neb* ('nose' or 'to be nosey'), *brambles* ('blackberries'), *bullets* ('sweets'), *skinch* ('truce'), *car/cuddy-handed* ('left-handed'), *loup* ('jump').

This is best done as a group activity, either by the class as a whole or by teams of five or more, as the results will be better if a large number of questionnaires are returned.

The questionnaire that Burbano-Elizondo used for her study is reproduced in Text 7: Dialect Questionnaire. Unless you live in the North East of England, you will need to adapt this by making a list of 'traditional' dialect words from your own area. You can do this either by asking older friends and relatives for dialect words that they remember, or by using a dialect dictionary from your region. Many of these were compiled in the late nineteenth/early twentieth centuries, and they can often be found in local libraries. Failing that, you may find that there are websites that provide lists of dialect words (see the resource guide on p. 108).

Give the questionnaire out to people of different ages, especially older people (ideally over 60) and younger people (under 20). You can start by asking your friends and relatives to help with this, and to pass questionnaires on to their friends. Usually, older people in particular are happy to take part in surveys like this, as they find them interesting and appreciate the interest in their local dialect. If you are unable to find enough contacts, you could ask local libraries for permission to leave copies for readers and pick them up later. If you have the facilities and expertise, you could even put the questionnaire on the web.

When you have a large enough number of responses (at least 20 from older people and 20 from younger people):

◎   Calculate for each person how many 'correct' responses there were.

◎   Work out an average for each age group.

◎   If you have enough questionnaires, you could also calculate averages for males/females in each age group.

◎   Work out which words, if any, are most likely still to be known by younger people, i.e. which have the most 'correct' responses.

◎   Work out which words, if any, are least likely still to be known by younger people, i.e. which have the least 'correct' responses.

57

Text 7: Dialect Questionnaire

Questionnaire

Full name: _____

Age: _____

Male ☐ / Female ☐

Place of birth: _____

INSTRUCTIONS:

✓ Before beginning to answer the questionnaire, do not forget to complete the section above with your personal details.
✓ When completing the questionnaire, bear in mind that you are dealing with dialect words, that is, words that are typical of your area.
✓ Read each question carefully before answering it.
✓ Write down as many answers as you can think of whenever it is required.
✓ If you do not know the answer of a question, just mark the "I don't know"-option represented by (???)

Let's see if you know these dialect words !

1. What is a *gowk*?

   a. A hamster   b. A cuckoo   c. A pigeon   d. ???

2. What is a *cuddy*?

   a. A small bird   b. A donkey   c. A hug   d. ???

3. What is a *paddock*?

   a. A frog or toad   b. A narrow path   c. A parrot   d. ???

4 What do you call a small river?

   a. Burn   b. Beck   c. Pond   d. ???

5. What do you call these parts of the body? (Write all the words you can think of for each one)

   a. _____
   b. _____
   c. _____

6. What can you see in these flashcards? (Write as many words as you can think of)

   a. _____
   b. _____

7. What are you doing if you *hoy* a ball?

    a. bounce it   b. blow it up   c. throw it   d. ???

    And if you *chuck it*?

    a. bounce it   b. blow it up   c. throw it   d. ???

8. If a dog is *louping,* what is it doing?

    a. Turning around and around happily
    b. Jumping
    c. Digging a hole to hide a bone
    d. ???

9. What are your words for staying away from school without your parents or teachers' authorisation? (Give your own answers)

    _____

    _____

10. What do you call the things you are going to see? (Give as many answers as you can for each of them)

    a. _____

    b. _____

11. What do you think *gadgie* means?

    a. An old car   b. A hook   c. A bloke or   d. ???
                                             an old man

    And *bairn*?

    a. Garage   b. Child   c. An old horse   d. ???

12. If someone tells you that you are quite glaky, what is he calling you?

    a. Thick, stupid   b. Cheeky   c. Clown   d. ???

13. What do you call someone who writes with his left hand? (Give as many answers as possible).

    _____

    _____

14. What do you say to your friends in the middle of a game if you want to take some time out?

   a. I need a barley
   b. I need some overtime
   c. I need a skinch
   d. Others _____

15. What is a *netty*?

   a. A toilet   b. A laundry room   c. A small fishing net   d. ???

16. Can you think of any other words that you, your friends or people of your family use that are characteristic of the speech of the area where you live? Make a list with them and try to explain their meaning or give examples of situations where you would use them. You can discuss them with a partner.

   1. _____
   2. _____
   3. _____
   4. _____
   5. _____
   6. _____
   7. _____
   8. _____
   9. _____
   10. _____

(There is no commentary for this activity.)

When Burbano-Elizondo carried out her study of dialect use by high-school students in Newcastle and Sunderland, she investigated their 'active' knowledge of local vocabulary as well as their passive knowledge of traditional terms. To do this, she used a combination of flashcards with pictures of objects for which she wanted to know the local words; pointing at things; and asking direct questions. In order to discover the words that the students used in everyday talk, she concentrated on concepts that would be relevant to them. A typical question was:

> What are your words for staying away from school without your parents' or teachers' authorisation? (Give your own answers.)

This method was very successful, for she found that the students wrote down some words which had not been found in other surveys, such as *kets* (sweets) and *doll off* (play truant), both from students in Sunderland only. Both these words were 'new' to the researcher, and could not be found in dialect dictionaries. This does not necessarily mean that they are 'new' words: it may simply be the case that older surveys and dictionaries either did not record words with these meanings, and/or that they concentrated on rural dialects. However, it is certainly true that not all regional words are old: the local alternatives to *chav* listed earlier are all fairly recent, and there are other cases of new words being coined in a particular region, even if they later spread throughout the country. In the 1970s *lush* as a word used to describe something or somebody very desirable, was a local word used on Tyneside. I remember sometime in the 1980s watching the children's TV programme *Why Don't You*, which was broadcast in school holidays and presented by children from a different city each week. One week it was the turn of Liverpool, and the presenter introduced an item by saying: 'As the Newcastle gang say, it's lush.' Soon, the word was joining the host of synonyms for 'attractive' on the cover of *Smash Hits* and gained national currency. So, what was at first a dialect word, i.e. used in a restricted geographical area, became slang, which is defined by Julie Coleman as follows, along with **colloquialisms** and jargon:

> *Slang* terms are characteristically short-lived, and tend to be used by a closed group of people, often united by common interests. Each generation has its own slang of approval and disapproval.

> *Colloquialisms* are used in informal speech and writing; they are widely spread and widely understood. . . . Unlike *dialect*, [they are] not geographically restricted, except perhaps at a national level.

> *Jargon* is also used by sub-sections of society. It typically belongs to professions or interest groups, such as doctors or train enthusiasts, and allows its users to speak with precision about technical matters.

> (2004: 4)

Speakers often fail to distinguish, or are totally unaware of, which words are local and which are colloquial, slang or jargon. This was found by Carmen Llamas who, when conducting a study in Middlesbrough, asked participants to provide 'words you think are dialect words or are local to the area you are from' (1999: 112). They actually provided a very wide range of terms, not all of which were local. Llamas notes that 'informants' insights into which variants are considered local, as opposed to those which are more widely used can be revealed. For example, one informant claimed not to have inserted a variant for 'soft shoes worn by children for P.E.' because she 'couldn't think of another word for *sandshoes*' (1999: 103–104). In fact *sandshoes* is geographically restricted to the North East of England, but it seemed so 'normal' to this woman that she thought it was standard. The method that Llamas used to elicit words from her participants involved giving them a set of **Sense Relation Network** sheets (SRNs). These were developed by Llamas and have since been further refined by Lourdes Burbano-Elizondo, Esther Asprey and Kate Wallace for their research in Sunderland, the West Midlands and Southampton respectively. They are based on the idea of 'mental maps', in which concepts are grouped together in the way that they are linked in the mind. This means that one word will bring others to mind, and avoids the 'mind going blank' problem that can occur when direct questions are asked. SRNs are an excellent tool for a number of reasons:

- ◎ They allow informants to take their time. Typically, SRNs are left with them for at least a week, so that they can write down words whenever they think of them.

- ◎ They 'empower' the informant. S/he has control in contrast to, for instance, the *SED* where the fieldworker asked the questions and did the recording. When they feel empowered, groups of speakers who are normally reluctant to co-operate can provide very rich data.

- ◎ Follow-up interviews reveal differences in use between variant words for the same concept. Llamas notes that 'after having given the responses *twoc, tax, nick, skank* and *swipe* for the notion word "steal", two informants went on to discuss at length precisely what each term referred to and their ideas on the origins of the words' (1999: 104).

- ◎ They elicit both 'active' and 'passive' vocabulary, and follow-up interviews reveal informants' insights into the usage of different genders, age groups, etc. Llamas relates how two young male informants argued 'that they would never use the variant *bonny* for the notion word "attractive", it being an "old person's" word, and they would never use *canny-looking*, it being used by girls, opting themselves to use *nectar, sweet, fit* and *lush*' (1999: 104).

Dialect surveys such as the *SED* were concerned with recording 'traditional' vocabulary from older speakers and so would not have uncovered words such as *twoc* (from the legal term 'Taken Without Owner's Consent', used first in the North East to refer to car theft, but now used more generally to mean stealing). The SRN method allows us to discover the wealth of vocabulary that is being used today.

Activity

Make copies of the SRN shown in Text 8A: Sense Relation Network Sheet, Being, Saying and Doing, and ask at least two people to complete it. You should also ask them to complete a copy of the consent form, also reproduced in Text 8B: Confidentiality and Consent Form. Leave the SRNs with them for a week and then arrange to interview them. (If the two people know each other well, you can interview them together.) You should record the interview.

◎   If they have given several words for certain concepts, ask them when they would use each word, or whether some are words they have heard but would not use themselves.

◎   Ask them if there are any other words they can think of now, which they had not written down on the SRN, and make a note of these.

When you have collected the SRNs and recorded the interviews, make a list of the words for each notion. Do you think that they are local dialect, slang or colloquial? If you have access to dialect dictionaries, look up some of these, if not, look them up in the *OED*, preferably the online version. In class, compare the words that your informants provided. Is there any difference between words provided by older and younger people, males and females, different social groups?

Text 8A: Sense Relation Network Sheet, Being, Saying and Doing

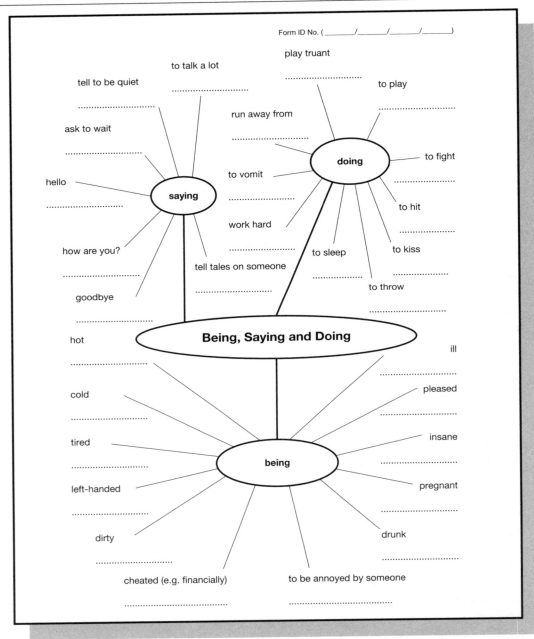

Form ID No. (_____ / _____ / _____ / _____)

play truant

to talk a lot

tell to be quiet

....

ask to wait

....

run away from

....

to play

....

doing

to fight

....

hello

saying

to vomit

....

to hit

work hard

how are you?

....

tell tales on someone

....

to sleep

....

to kiss

to throw

....

goodbye

....

hot

....

Being, Saying and Doing

ill

....

pleased

cold

....

....

insane

tired

....

being

left-handed

....

pregnant

dirty

....

drunk

....

cheated (e.g. financially)

to be annoyed by someone

....

....

Text 8B: Confidentiality and Consent Form

Confidentiality and Consent

As the instruction sheet explains, the purpose of this survey is to gather information about the way English is used in the British Isles today. In order to do this, I would like your permission to record the discussion about the sheets you have completed.

Use of Information

The information provided by you will be used to describe language in your area. It will be used for my project, and extracts may be included in my work, which will be seen by examiners. All the information you provide will remain completely anonymous.

By providing me with written and recorded information you indicate your consent to the collection, use, and electronic storage and processing of this information solely for the purposes described above in the section *Use of Information*

Signed..

Date..

(Under 18's only)

Parent/Guardian's signature....................................

Date..

(There is no commentary for this activity.)

SUMMARY

We began this unit with a discussion of the phenomenon of lexical attrition, whereby items of traditional dialect vocabulary are being lost to the younger generations. Research has shown that, while some words have been lost, especially those referring to objects and activities that no longer exist, such as farm implements or industrial processes, others, such as the different regional terms for a bread roll, are still used even by young people. In fact, young people are still introducing new regional dialect terms, such as the various words for *chav* found in different parts of Britain. We discussed the difference between *dialect*, *slang*, *jargon* and *colloquialisms*, but noted that speakers are often unaware of the differences between these. Finally, a questionnaire and a Sense Relation Network Sheet (SRN) were introduced, the former for use in researching speakers' knowledge of dialect words (passive vocabulary), the latter for eliciting all the words used by a speaker for key concepts (active vocabulary).

Extension

Using the information from the two activities in this unit, compile a glossary of local dialect words, either as a booklet or as a website. If you produce a booklet, you may want to offer a copy to your local library.

Regional grammar

In the previous units, we have looked at regional accents and at regional vocabulary. Dialects also differ from one another in terms of grammar: the ways in which words and sentences are put together. Take the following sentences:

1   Are yous going out tonight?

2   We might could do with some washing powder.

3   I'll see you at the Christmas.

4   We're open nine while five.

5   I tret myself to a new dress.

Although these sentences only contain Standard English vocabulary, they all contain non-standard grammar. If a speaker of another language produced them in an English test, they would probably all be marked 'wrong', yet sentences like these are used by native speakers of English, so how can they be incorrect? Many people who are happy to accept regional accents and even dialect words, consider the use of dialectal grammar to be 'wrong' or 'uneducated', but it is important to bear in mind the difference between non-standard and **sub-standard** when discussing regional dialects. Jenny Cheshire and Jim Milroy explain this difference using an analogy to tools:

The term *standardization* can be used of phenomena outside language and means the imposition of uniformity upon a class of objects. Thus, we may describe a set of motor-car components, or electric plugs, or a coinage system, as being 'standardized'. When such objects are described as 'sub-standard', the implication is that they are not of the quality required to perform their function in the most reliable way. . . . When, on the other hand, we speak of items as *non-standard*, there is no such value-judgement. The best analogy here is with hand-made, as against factory, tools. Whereas factories produce large numbers of items (e.g. spades) that are all identical, those made by traditional craftsmen are all slightly different.

(1993: 3–4)

The point here is that a non-standard tool may actually be more appropriate for certain jobs, but a sub-standard one will not perform as well for any job. If we look at the sentences listed earlier, the same argument can be applied. Sentence 1 was (and often is) addressed to myself and my husband by my older daughter, who grew up in Newcastle. The form *yous* is a plural, so I know when she says this that she is addressing both of us and wants to know whether she will have the house to herself. Had she been addressing me alone, she would have said: 'Are *you* going out tonight?' When it comes to second-person **pronouns** (*you*, etc.), the Newcastle dialect, along with several other urban varieties of British English, Irish English and some US and Australian varieties, 'does the job' better than Standard English, which, unlike French, German, Spanish and, indeed, Irish, has only one form for the singular and plural, so that, without eye contact, or phrases such as 'you guys', it is impossible to tell in some situations whether the speaker is addressing one or more people. Standard English was able to make this distinction until about the seventeenth century: *you* was the plural form and *thee/thou* the singular forms. However, *you* came to be used as a polite way of addressing a single person (like French *vous*) and *thee/thou* died out of Standard usage. Some dialects still use *thee* and *thou* (in fact, there is a phrase in South Yorkshire '*thee-ing and tha-ing*' which means speaking in dialect), but this is becoming rare. Speakers of modern dialects tend to use *yous* or, in the Southern states of the US, *you all* to mark the plural. Who can say that any of these forms are 'wrong' when they make a grammatical distinction (singular versus plural) that Standard English can only achieve through circumlocution?

The other sentences in the earlier list contain examples of non-standard usage that are legitimate constructions but simply different from Standard English. Sentence 2 will look very strange to most readers because it contains two **modal** verbs. Modals in English are a small set of verbs which express concepts such as possibility (*can, could*), obligation (*must, should*), futurity (*will, shall*), possibility (*may, might*), hypothetical circumstances (*should, would*), etc. They behave differently to other verbs in that:

◎ They form the negative without *do*. I *can't* or I *cannot*, but not I *walkn't* or I *walk not* (except in archaic language).

◎ They form the **interrogative** (questions) without *do*. *Can you?* or *Could you?* but not *Walk you?* (except in archaic language).

◎ They can be used as a substitute (code) to avoid repeating another verb. *If you won't answer the door, then I will.*

◎ They can be used for emphasis *You shall go to the ball!*

These four properties of modals (as well as the **auxiliary verbs** *be, do* and *have*) are often referred to as the NICE properties, standing for Negative, Interrogative, Code and Emphasis. However, Standard English has other rules regarding modals, one of which is that only one can appear in each **clause**. The reason why sentence 2 looks so strange to speakers of Standard English and most dialects is that it contains two modals *might* and *could*. This is known as a 'double modal' and means something like: 'I think there is a possibility that we might need some washing powder.' Since *might* already introduces the idea of possibility, *could* seems redundant, but it is really a way of being very tentative and polite. 'Double modal' constructions such as *might could* (which is by far the most common), —*'ll can, might should* and *might would* are found in Scots, Northumbrian and the dialects of the Appalachians in the Southern states of the US.

Sentence 3 may look strange because it has the **definite article** *the* before a **proper noun** *Christmas*. In Standard English, *the* is used to specify which of a number of possible things, etc. is being referred to, as in 'I'd like the blue shirt, please', referring to a very specific shirt, as opposed to 'I'd like *a* blue shirt', which could refer to any from a number of shirts. Since Christmas comes but once a year, Standard English does not normally use any article before it, though you could say 'I'd like a Christmas without a family row', for instance. Several dialects of English have different rules for the use of *the*: in these dialects, it can be used with names of seasons (*Christmas, Easter, Autumn, Summer*); illnesses (*chicken pox, measles*); institutions (*hospital, school*), etc. Dialects in which *the* occurs before such words include those of Ireland, Scotland, Northumberland and Tyneside.

Sentence 4 is so common in Yorkshire that people who live there tend not to recognise it as non-standard. Here *while* means the same as Standard English *until*. There is a joke/urban legend that a new traffic system in Halifax caused accidents because the sign stated 'do not cross while red light shows'. In Standard English, this sentence means the pedestrian should wait until the red light has gone, but in Yorkshire, it means he or she should only cross when the light is red.

Sentence 5 contains a different past tense form of the verb *treat* to that found in Standard English. Verbs in English have their past tense forms either using the regular (sometimes known as weak) method, in which *–ed* is added: *walk/walked; shop/shopped; treat/treated*; or according to various irregular or strong patterns, involving changes in the vowel: *meet/met; swim/swam; take/took*. Non-standard dialects sometimes use a weak form where Standard English has a strong one, as in *sayed* for Standard *said*, and sometimes the other way round, as in *tret*. Since *meet/met* is an acceptable pattern in Standard English, why should the same pattern in *treat/tret* be seen as 'wrong'? In fact *tret* is found in a number of Northern English dialects.

It would be impossible in a book of this size to discuss all the features of regional English grammar, but the checklist on pp. 78–80 will give you a good idea of what to look for in your own region. All the non-standard forms in sentences 1–5 earlier are found in specific regional dialects, mainly those of Scotland, Ireland and the North of England, but there are some patterns that are found in non-standard usage throughout and sometimes beyond the UK. These are often highly stigmatised, and are considered to be sub-standard by non-linguists, but there is nothing inherently 'wrong' with them, and they can often be found in the works of celebrated authors from earlier times. A good example of this is the so-called **double** or **multiple negative**, found in sentences such as:

6   They never learned you nowt (*nowt* = 'nothing').

7   I was never no good after that.

Both these sentences are taken from the *Newcastle Electronic Corpus of Tyneside English* (*NECTE*), details of which are provided on p. 108. They were recorded in 1969, from working-class speakers who had left school at what was then the legal minimum age of 15. Both speakers are talking freely about their negative experiences at school, where sentences such as 6 and 7 would certainly have been condemned by teachers as 'wrong'. In earlier English, before the eighteenth century, 'double negatives' were perfectly respectable: Shakespeare has four negatives in one line in *Twelfth Night*:

I have one heart, one bosom, and one truth,
And that *no* woman has, *nor never none*
Shall mistress be of it, save I alone.

Here 'nor never none' just emphasises the speaker's determination never to give his heart to a woman, but today this would be seen as non-standard. The 'double negative' is one of a number of structures condemned by eighteenth-century grammar-writers as 'illogical'. It was first mentioned by Greenwood, who stated that 'two *Negatives*, or two *Adverbs* of Denying, do in *English* affirm' (1711: 160). 'Two negatives make a positive' is a rule that works in mathematics, but not in language: in French, constructions such as *ne . . . jamais* ('not never') are standard and in most varieties of English, double or multiple negation is used for emphasis. They are more likely to be used by less educated speakers simply because they have been marked 'wrong' by so many generations of teachers that more educated speakers have learnt to avoid them. The same can be said for 'double comparative' and 'double superlative' constructions such as:

8   Because you were more fitter.

9   She's got the most loveliest clothes.

Sentence 8 was taken from a study of Bolton (Shorrocks 1999), sentence 9 from a study of children's usage in the North East of England (McDonald 1980), but either could have been heard anywhere in the UK. In Standard English, the **comparative** (comparing two things, people, etc.) can be expressed either by placing *more* in front of an **adjective** or **adverb** as in *Volvos are more reliable than Hondas* or *Volvos run more efficiently than Hondas* or, where the adjective/adverb has only one or two syllables, by adding *-er*, as in *Porsches are smarter than Volvos* or *Porsches go faster than Volvos*. Likewise, the **superlative** in which more than two are compared and one described as 'the most', either *most* or *-est* can be used, as in *Volvos are the most reliable cars* or *Porsches are the smartest cars* etc. In non-standard English, both methods can be used for emphasis as in sentences 8 and 9. As with the double negative, these forms were common in Standard English before the eighteenth century. Both constructions are used by well-known authors: Ben Jonson in *Cataline* writes 'Contain your spirit in more stricter bounds,' while Shakespeare's *Julius Caesar* says 'This was the most unkindest cut of all.' Features such as double negatives, comparatives and superlatives may be found in almost any region, so they are not really 'regional' in the same way as, say, double modals are, but non-standard features such as these are more likely to be used by the same speakers who use other dialect features, and so are worth noting.

For many years, dialect study tended to concentrate on features of accent or vocabulary, with little attention paid to grammar. The prevailing view was that dialects of English all shared more or less the same 'grammar', with only trivial differences between them. Several studies from the 1980s onwards, listed on pp. 105–108, have investigated the grammatical features of regional dialects in the UK, and we now know that there are striking differences between dialects, some of which could lead to misunderstandings between speakers from different regions. For instance, in Newcastle 'You haven't got to do that' means you *must not* but in Standard English and most other dialects it means *you are not obliged to* do it. So, a person from London, on being told by a Geordie 'You haven't got to shut that door', might reply 'It's OK, I'll shut it anyway'. The cautionary tale of the Halifax traffic lights is another example of such a cross-dialectal misunderstanding: it is not only the British and the Americans who are 'divided by a common language'. Other features of dialect grammar may not cause misunderstandings, but can seem very strange to speakers of other dialects. The 'double modal' construction is one example of this, another is the gender system of some traditional dialects in the South West of England and in Newfoundland (a part of Canada settled by speakers from Dorset). English, unlike many other European languages, has a system of **natural gender**: with a few exceptions, such as ships and, for some speakers cars, inanimate objects and most animals are referred to as *it*; male humans and male animals that are important to humans (pets, horses, etc.) are referred to as *he*, and female humans and 'special' animals are referred to as *she*. In German and many other European languages, there is **grammatical gender**: words take the masculine, feminine or neuter pronoun according to the grammatical class of the word. Thus, the word for *girl* is *das Mädchen*, which takes the neuter form *das* of the word for 'the', rather than the feminine form *die*, simply because all nouns with the ending -*chen* (meaning 'little', rather like the -*ie* in words such as *doggie*) are classed as neuter. Old English (before the Norman Conquest) had such a system, but it gradually died out in most varieties of English. In the South West of England and Newfoundland, a trace of this old system remains: nouns such as *car, cow, bucket, shovel, tree, flower* take the pronoun *he*; those such as *boy, father, uncle, nephew, man* also take *he*, while only nouns referring to human females, such as *girl, mother, aunt, niece, woman* take *she*. There is a great deal of work to be done investigating regional dialect grammar, but carrying out research of this kind is not straightforward.

One reason why research into dialect grammar has been neglected in the past is that many of the features discussed above are unlikely to occur in interviews, or are rare because the occasion for using them doesn't often arise. If a researcher interviews one person at a time, that person will never need to use the plural form *yous*, simply because he or she is only talking to one person. Likewise, regional forms of interrogatives (questions) are not likely to be heard in interviews when the researcher is asking all the questions. The 'double modal' construction discussed earlier is rarely heard on Tyneside, but this does not necessarily mean that it is disappearing: there are simply not many occasions when it is needed. So, a researcher could record many hours of speech and still not find any examples of the fascinating grammatical structure that he or she had overheard on the bus. To overcome this problem, we have to use questionnaires that either ask informants to supply the form that they would use in a particular sentence, or that provide a list of 'dialect' sentences and ask whether the informant has heard these constructions and/or would use them. An example of the former is the questionnaire used by the *SED*, in which informants might be asked to 'complete' a sentence such as:

> That's the chap . . . uncle drowned.

This was intended to provide different forms for Standard English *whose*: some informants gave forms such as *whaes*, or *whats*, while others changed the sentence to, for instance *that's the chap, tha knows, his uncle drowned* or *that's the chap as his uncle drowned*. In either case, the question succeeded in providing regional alternatives for the Standard English *whose*. Such methods have been criticised on the grounds that informants may feel that they are being 'tested' and so may not give 'natural' responses, but the *SED* collected a lot of useful evidence in this way. Now that we have a number of studies of regional grammar, a second type of questionnaire is useful for establishing the extent to which certain features are used by different age groups, genders or social groups, or how widespread they are across geographical regions. Cheshire, Edwards and Whittle devised a 'child-friendly' questionnaire for use in a survey carried out in schools between 1986 and 1989. The questionnaire was illustrated with amusing cartoons, and required the children (working in groups) to tick boxes next to forms that they had heard in their local community. The children had been prepared for this task by a series of 'language awareness' lessons so the results (reported in Cheshire, Edwards and Whittle (1993)), were very useful in providing a 'snapshot' of regional variation in grammar. The best way to investigate regional grammar is to combine the study of speech from interviews or recorded conversations with evidence from a questionnaire.

Activity

The extracts shown in Text 9: Interviews in Tyneside and Sheffield are taken from interviews recorded in Gateshead (Tyneside) in 1969 (A) and in Sheffield in 1981 (B). Both speakers are female and working class. Using the checklist on pp. 78–80, identify any non-standard features of grammar used by these speakers. Are there some features used by both speakers, which we might consider 'Northern' features, and others which are more specific to either Tyneside or Sheffield? (Note, the sentences are taken from different parts of each interview and don't follow on from each other. No attempt has been made to reproduce the accent here so in A, *know* was pronounced /naː/, but this is irrelevant to the study of grammar.)

Text 9: Interviews in Tyneside and Sheffield

A

I lived in there for about, oh, eighteen or nineteen year . . . maybe a little bit longer, I divn't know, but er then I come ower here 'cos they were modernising the flats you-see.

He was in the hospital for six month and he never worked no more.

Well, he was old then, when he was born, and when Jimmy was only about the twenty-two, his grandfather was eighty odd then.

Wor Thomas'll be fourteen at Christmas Day, and wor little Steven, that's the seventh, he'll be ten in January the sixteenth.

That was for me for to get bread in for the bairns.

B

My mother come from Walkley and my dad come from Huddersfield so I'm half-and-half and I've always lived at Hillsborough up to this last thirty year and I've come to live down here.

My second husband was a labourer he did owt, he worked in t'brickyard.

Well both lads have got made redundant, love. One worked in rolling mill from being fourteen at Hallamshire Steel and File, well Neils took it over and er when they found out they could buy steel cheaper abroad than what they do it in Sheffield so he's been made redundant and he's worked from being fourteen up to forty-eight in steel-works slogging hard love, never had much time off work and other one he was apprenticeship – ooh now then mechanic in steel-works he took his dad's job.

I'm not harmed nowt with been working all these years I've brought a family up and worked.

I've a clock-radio and we listen to Radio Sheffield to all news what's going off.

When it was snowing she couldn't get no buses and when strike were on you couldn't get could you?

(See the commentary on p. 94.)

(See the commentary on p. 94.)

Activity

The questionnaire shown in Text 10: Language Questionnaire was used by Lourdes Burbano-Elizondo for her research in Sunderland. It is designed to enable the researcher to find out what regional dialect features are used in a certain area and by whom. Some of the examples here, such as 22–24, would not be found outside the North East of England, so you will need to adapt the questionnaire so that it includes features that are more typical of the region that you wish to investigate.

This would work best as a class or group project. Each individual should give the questionnaire to at least four people (one older male, one younger male, one older female, one younger female) but 'the more the merrier'. When the completed questionnaires have been returned, you should each do the following calculations for your own material, then bring them together to form a single survey.

◎ How many regional dialect features are used by each group of speakers (older males, younger females etc.)? Is there a clear pattern of use by one age group or gender?

◎ How many features are known but not used? Again, how does this correlate with age and gender?

◎ Which features are known and/or used most widely? Are these very specifically regional features or non-standard features that are very widespread?

◎ Which features are used by only a small number of people? Would these be considered 'old fashioned'?

If you have collected questionnaires from different regions, or even from different towns or villages within the same wider region, you may want to discuss any differences between these.

Text 10: Language Questionnaire

Language Questionnaire

Please, tick more than one box if necessary. Feel free to write any comments by the sentences.

Tick (✔) this box if you would hear this in Sunderland	Tick (✔) this box if you would use this type of sentence yourself in speech.	Tick (✔) this box if you would use this type of sentence when writing to a friend.

1. ❑❑❑ When are yous two going home?
2. ❑❑❑ What are thou/tha doing?
3. ❑❑❑ Ye can get lost, Kevin!
4. ❑❑❑ Give us a pen, I want to write a letter
5. ❑❑❑ Us'll do it.
6. ❑❑❑ This is wor car.
7. ❑❑❑ This is me cup.
8. ❑❑❑ Give I a cup of tea!
9. ❑❑❑ Them shoes there are very expensive.
10. ❑❑❑ My friend came to visit me last week lives in France.
11. ❑❑❑ The radio what I bought yesterday isn't working properly.
12. ❑❑❑ The man what I was talking to is my boss.
13. ❑❑❑ You know me cousin that her husband died?
14. ❑❑❑ My cousin which got married last year is getting divorced.
15. ❑❑❑ Would you like a chocolate? Yes, I'll have a one.
16. ❑❑❑ Their new house is much more bigger than the old one.
17. ❑❑❑ These are the most beautifullest paintings I've ever seen.
18. ❑❑❑ This is geet hard, Sir.
19. ❑❑❑ They're useless, them.
20. ❑❑❑ Never mind, I'll manage but.
21. ❑❑❑ I've never heard of him like.
22. ❑❑❑ I do all the work, dinnet I?
23. ❑❑❑ I dinnet like him.
24. ❑❑❑ Ye divvent like him, div ye?
25. ❑❑❑ There was ten kids playing in the street.
26. ❑❑❑ The carpets was soaked.
27. ❑❑❑ They was soaking.
28. ❑❑❑ I can't find nothing in this mess.

29. ❑❑❑ They said they were coming back on Monday and they never.
30. ❑❑❑ I'll put the kettle on, for to make some tea?
31. ❑❑❑ With the wife being ill, I had to stay in and look after her.
32. ❑❑❑ Joe can-t come tomorrow, being as he's working late.
33. ❑❑❑ The house needs painted.
34. ❑❑❑ You can't eat sweets in lessons, can't you not?
35. ❑❑❑ He can't come to the party, can he not?
36. ❑❑❑ She can come, can she not?
37. ❑❑❑ He is coming, isn't he?
38. ❑❑❑ You could say it could you?
39. ❑❑❑ She once asked me did it interfere with me.
40. ❑❑❑ When he discovered I wasn't at school he wanted to know what was the matter.
41. ❑❑❑ Can I come in?
42. ❑❑❑ Will I open the window?
43. ❑❑❑ He must can do it
44. ❑❑❑ He wouldn't could've worked, even if you had asked him.
45. ❑❑❑ I can't play on Friday. I work late. I might could get it changed, though.
46. ❑❑❑ John mustn't be at home because he doesn't answer the phone.
47. ❑❑❑ That traffic sign means that you haven't got to park here.
48. ❑❑❑ You don't have to come if you don't want to.
49. ❑❑❑ I've broke a plate.
50. ❑❑❑ I come this morning, but you weren-t in.
51. ❑❑❑ He done it all right.
52. ❑❑❑ I had forgotten to buy the onions.
53. ❑❑❑ He give us a pound for doing it.
54. ❑❑❑ We had went to the coast for the day.
55. ❑❑❑ I seen Albert on Tuesday.
56. ❑❑❑ We usually gan down the pub on Thursday's.
57. ❑❑❑ I knew a bloke who were doing speech therapy.
58. ❑❑❑ We was walking along the road when it happened.
59. ❑❑❑ It were too cold out.
60. ❑❑❑ You wasn't listening to what I said.

(There is no commentary for this activity.)

SUMMARY

In this unit we have introduced the characteristic features of regional grammar in British dialects. More widespread features such as multiple negation have been discussed, along with the popular notion that such features are not dialect, but 'bad grammar'. There has been some discussion of the history of these features, showing that many of these were used in earlier literature, and the notion that dialects 'have' grammar, and are not 'ungrammatical'. We have discussed the difficulties of collecting data on dialect grammar, and introduced a questionnaire devised for the Survey of Regional English.

Extension

Compile a grammar of the dialect of your region, using the results of the questionnaires collected for the previous activity, along with any information on your regional dialect that you can find in books, articles and websites. You can also consider whether you would use constructions different from Standard English (introspection). Use the following checklist to help you decide what to include. When you have completed this dialect grammar, you could produce either a pamphlet/book or a website to make this available to other people in your area who might be interested.

Checklist of regional grammar features

Verbs

◎ Irregular verbs (make a table of these, showing the infinitive, past tense and past participle forms, such as *sing, sang, sung*).

◎ Do you use *was* with plural **subjects** ('We/they was soaked') or *were* with singular subjects ('I/he/she were soaked')?

◎ Concord: do you have constructions such as 'they was lucky' or 'the carpets was wet'?

◎ Modal verbs: do you have 'double modals'? Are modals such as *shall, should* avoided? Can *must not/mustn't* mean 'the evidence leads me to believe that . . . not'?

◎ Negatives: is multiple negation common? Do you have auxiliary **contraction** (He'll not come) or negative contraction (He won't come)?

◎ Can 'for to' introduce an infinitive, as in 'I'm waiting for to catch the bus'? Does it always mean 'in order to'?

◎ After *need* and *want* do you use the past participle ('My hair needs washed') or the present participle ('My hair needs washing') or the passive ('My hair needs to be washed')?

◎ Interrogatives: what tag questions are used? Is the same tag used whatever the verb in the main clause, as in 'I'm going home now, innit'? Are different tags used depending on whether the speaker expects a 'yes' or 'no' answer, as in 'You can swim, can't you'? (expecting yes) vs. 'You can't swim, can you'? (expecting no) and 'You can swim, can you?' (not sure of the answer).

◎ Are the auxiliary and verb inverted in indirect questions, as in 'I asked him was he going' vs. Standard English 'I asked him if he was going'?

Nouns and pronouns

◎ What personal pronouns are used? Are *thee/thou* used for second person singular? Is *yous* used for second person plural? Are there any other forms that differ from Standard English?

◎ Do you use himself/themselves or hisself/theirselves?

◎ Is the **object** form used in compound subjects, such as 'Me and my brother went home'?

◎ Do you use **pronoun exchange**, i.e. subject form in object position and vice versa, as in 'Her said to I'?

◎ Is grammatical gender used at all, i.e. *him* or *her* to refer to inanimate objects, etc.?

◎ What relative pronouns are used? Are *wh-* relatives (*who, whom, whose, which*) used frequently? Are *what, as* or *at* used as relative markers, as in 'The play what I wrote'? Can the relative be missed out in subject position, as in 'There's a girl lives next to the sweet shop'.

◎ Is the definite article reduced or omitted, as in 'It's in t'kitchen' or 'It's in kitchen'? Is the definite article used where it would not be used in Standard English as in 'I'll see you at the Christmas'?

◎ Is the plural marker omitted after numbers with nouns of measure, as in *three mile, six pint*?

Adjectives

◎ Are double comparatives and/or superlatives used?

◎ What intensifiers are used (*right* good, *proper* stupid, *well* angry, etc.)?

Adverbs

◎ Are adverbs without *-ly* used, as in 'Do it careful'?

Prepositions

◎ Are these used differently from Standard English, e.g. 'I got it off my dad' (SE 'from'), 'on a weekend' (SE 'at the weekend'), 'open 9 while 5' (SE 9 till 5) etc.?

Discourse features

◎ Is right dislocation as in 'He's stupid, he is', or 'He's stupid, him' used?

◎ Is left dislocation as in 'Him, he's stupid' used?

◎ What endearment terms (*love, pet, duck*, etc. are used)?

◎ Are any focusing devices used, such as *like* ('Are you coming, like?'), *see* ('See me, I'm mental'), etc.?

This is not a definitive list: you may find features or constructions not included here. It is just intended to provide a guide to the kind of features you should look for.

seven

Writing in dialect

In Unit two, we looked at some examples of dialect use in advertising, the tourist industry and on the internet. We saw that, in these contexts, dialect tends to be used for humorous purposes, and the representation of dialect draws on stereotypes, using semi-phonetic spelling to indicate the best-known features of the accent concerned, along with dialect words and features of grammar. In this unit, we will look at the ways in which more literary authors represent dialect: where the author's intention is humorous, the techniques used are often the same as those employed by the writers of the texts discussed in Unit two. However, some authors use more sophisticated methods to present a fuller picture of the dialect concerned.

Since the late fifteenth century, it has been normal for authors writing in English to use the Standard form of the language, which first developed at that time. In earlier periods, writers had used their own regional dialect, so that a text written in the West Midlands would be noticeably different from one written in the South. When William Caxton introduced printing to England in 1476, he realised that, in order to make the publication of books financially viable, they would have to be written in a form of English that could be understood throughout the nation. In the preface to his translation of Virgil's *Aeneid* from Latin into English, Caxton complains of what he calls the 'diversity and change of language' and that 'that common English that is spoken in one shire varieth from another' (everyday English varies from one county to the next) (Caxton

(1490), cited in Freeborn (1998: 261)). However, his complaints were written in the Standard English that was already beginning to be used by civil servants to ensure that official documents would be understood throughout the country. Caxton's decision to use this form of English meant that, from that point on, authors would only use dialect consciously and for specific purposes, the norm being to write in Standard English. Shakespeare was born in Warwickshire, but his plays show hardly any trace of his origins because they were written for the London stage. Shakespeare did make use of dialect in some of his plays, but always to make a specific point or create an effect.

Before we go on to consider the techniques used by literary authors and the intended effects of their use of dialect, we need to make a distinction between literary dialect, in which the majority of the text is in Standard English, but the speech of some characters is represented as dialectal, and dialect literature, where the whole text, or at least most of it, is written in dialect. When Shakespeare represents certain characters in *Henry V* as speaking in Welsh, Scottish and Irish varieties of English, this is literary dialect, because everybody else in the play (except the French princess) is represented as speaking Standard English. Likewise, novelists such as Charles Dickens write in Standard English except that the dialogue of some characters such as Sam Weller in *The Pickwick Papers* is represented as 'Cockney'. The poems of Robert Burns and William Barnes, on the other hand, are examples of dialect literature, because they are written wholly in dialect, to the extent that notes and glossaries are needed by readers who are not familiar with Scots or Dorset dialect. (There is an issue here about whether Scots should be considered a language or a dialect, but, at the time when Burns was writing, works published in Scotland would normally be written in Standard English, so his decision to use Scots was a deliberate act of rebellion.)

The main problem for any author wishing to represent a non-standard dialect is the need to strike a balance between accuracy and accessibility. If too many 'non-standard' features are used, the text may be difficult to read, especially for readers who are unfamiliar with the dialect portrayed, but the author needs to make the dialect recognisable as such. If the text is intended for a local readership, the author can afford to give a much fuller portrayal of the dialect. Irvine Welsh's novel *Trainspotting* has enjoyed global success, despite the fact that much of it is written in the urban Scots dialect of Edinburgh. However, while the use of dialect in *Trainspotting* has been the subject of a great deal of comment, if we look at an extract we can see that not every word, or even every sentence, is written in dialect.

Text 11: *Trainspotting*

Sick Boy tourniqued Ali above her elbow, obviously staking his place in the queue, and tapped up a vein *oan* her thin ash-white *airm.*

— Want me *tae dae* it? he asked.

She nodded.

He *droaps* a cotton ball *intae* the spoon *n blaws oan* it, before sucking up *aboot* 5 mls through the needle, *intae* the barrel *ay* the syringe. He's *goat* a *fuckin* huge blue vein tapped up, which seems *tae* be almost *comin* through Ali's *airm.* He pierces her flesh and injects a *wee* bit slowly, before sucking blood back *intae* the chamber. Her lips are quivering as she gazes pleadingly at him for a second or two. Sick Boy's face looks ugly, leering and reptilian, before he slams the cocktail towards her brain.

(Welsh 2004: 8–9)

Commentary

The first line of Text 11: *Trainspotting* is written entirely in Standard English, and the only indication of Scots in the first sentence is in the spellings <oan> and <airm>. Throughout this extract, the spelling <oa> is used for Standard English <o> in <oan> <droaps> and <goat>. Both this and <airm> are examples of semi-phonetic spelling: the spellings warn the reader that the pronunciation is different from that of RP and indicate how the words would be pronounced in Scots, with a longer vowel, since <oa> and <ai> in Standard English spelling usually represent the vowels or diphthongs found in *goat* and *air* respectively. These spellings don't really cause too much difficulty for readers who are unfamiliar with Scots, because in each case only one extra letter is added, and the context helps to identify the words. The word between 'vein' and 'her thin ash-white airm' is most likely to be 'on', and, given the context of Sick boy having 'tourniqued above her elbow', the last word in this sentence must be 'arm'. Other examples of semi-phonetic spelling here are <tae>, <dae>and <intae>, for 'to', 'do' and 'into' and <aboot> for 'about', none of which should cause any difficulty for the reader. The spellings <comin> and <fuckin> for 'coming' and 'fucking', suggest the pronunciation /ɪn/ for RP /ɪŋ/, but Welsh does not use this semi-phonetic spelling for all words with this ending: <sucking> appears twice in this extract, never <suckin>, and likewise <quivering> and <leering> are spelt as in Standard English. It is clear from this extract that Irvine Welsh uses semi-phonetic spelling quite sparingly, and mainly on more common words which the reader will have no problem identifying. The intention is not to produce a novel written entirely in Scots, but to provide enough pointers to urban Scots to 'place' his setting and characters. Apart from the word *wee* in 'a wee bit slowly', all the vocabulary in this extract is Standard English, as is the grammar. Elsewhere in the novel, Scots words are used, such as *bairn* for 'child' and more specifically Edinburgh dialect words such as *schemie* for a lower-class person or 'chav', who lives in one of the local authority housing 'schemes'. However, Welsh's use of Scots is not at all dense: Text 11 contains 128 words, only 18 of which are in any way non-standard. To put it another way, 86 per cent of Text 11 is in Standard English, yet Welsh has clearly succeeded in giving the reader the 'flavour' of urban Scots. As such, *Trainspotting* is a good example of literary dialect, in which much of the writing is in Standard English, but the author makes selective use of dialect to achieve a specific effect.

The main technique used by Irvine Welsh is semi-phonetic spelling, but other authors may use eye-dialect, **allegro speech respellings** and **regionalisms**. Eye-dialect is used when the author wishes to give an impression of non-standard and/or uneducated speech. Spellings such as <wot> for 'what' represent pronunciations which would be used by RP-speakers, /wɒt/, but the 'deviant' spelling gives an impression of uneducated, or, at least, very informal usage. Allegro speech respellings represent the way words tend to be shortened when we speak quickly. Examples of this are <an> for 'and' or <cos> for 'because'. In Text 12: *Tommy*, the poet Rudyard Kipling makes use of both eye-dialect and allegro speech respellings to represent the language of the lower classes. The narrator of the poem, 'Tommy Atkins' is meant to represent the ordinary, working-class 'squaddie', who is thrown out of pubs as a troublemaker in peacetime, but hailed as a hero in war.

Text 12: *Tommy*

I **WENT** into a public-'ouse to get a pint o' beer,
The publican 'e up an' sez, "We serve no red-coats here."
The girls be'ind the bar they laughed an' giggled fit to die,
I outs into the street again an' to myself sez I:

O it's Tommy this, an' Tommy that, an' 'Tommy, go away';
But it's 'Thank you, Mister Atkins', when the band begins
   to play, –
The band begins to play, my boys, the band begins to play,
O it's 'Thank you, Mister Atkins', when the band begins
   to play.

(http://whitewolf.newcastle.edu.au/words)

Commentary

Here, Kipling uses an apostrophe to mark any 'missing' letter, but it is important to distinguish the semi-phonetic spelling in <'ouse>, <'e> and <be'ind> for 'house', 'he' and 'behind', from the allegro speech respelling in <an'> for 'and' and <o'> for 'of'. The first of these shows 'h-dropping', which, although very common in England, is still regional and, in this case, probably Cockney, but the second represents a kind of pronunciation which even RP-speakers would use in rapid, colloquial speech. Eye-dialect is used in the spelling <sez>, which represents a pronunciation /sɛz/ which would be used even by RP-speakers. (Of course, in the fourth line, 'sez I' also represents non-standard grammar, 'says I' where Standard English would have 'I said'.) The poet's intention is not so much to give an accurate portrayal of any particular accent and/or dialect as to provide a flavour of the colloquial non-standard English of the common soldier. Note that the 'publican' is represented as using Standard English, with no 'h-dropping': 'We serve no red-coats here.'

Where an author intends to provide a fuller and more accurate representation of a specific dialect, he or she may use regionalisms. These are usually words or grammatical features with a regional distribution, such as we have discussed in Units five and six. Text 13: *North and South* is taken from Chapter 7 of Elizabeth Gaskell's novel *North and South*, in which the author highlights the difference between the 'soft' life of the South and the harsh conditions in the cotton mills of Lancashire. The novel's heroine, Margaret, has moved from the South of England to 'Darkshire', a fictional city that represents Manchester. She befriends Betty and her father Nicholas, both of whom work in the cotton mill. In this extract they discuss 'trouble up t'mill', the threat of industrial action.

Text 13: *North and South*

'Ay,' said he. 'That there strike was badly managed. Folk got into th' management of it, as were either fools or not true men. Yo'll see, it'll be different this time.'

'But all this time you've not told me what you're striking for,' said Margaret, again.

'Why, yo' see, there's five or six masters who have set themselves again paying the wages they've been paying these two years past, and flourishing upon, and getting richer upon. And now they come to us, and say we're to take less. And we won't. We'll just clem them to death first; and see who'll work for 'em then. They'll have killed the goose that laid 'em the golden eggs, I reckon.'

'And so you plan dying, in order to be revenged upon them!'

'No,' said he, 'I dunnot. I just look forward to the chance of dying at my post sooner than yield. That's what folk call fine and honourable in a soldier, and why not in a poor weaver-chap?'

Commentary

Elizabeth Gaskell's representation of Nicholas's speech contains the allegro speech respelling <'em> for 'them', but the spelling of 'the' as <th'> is a regionalism, marking as it does the reduction of the definite article to /θ/ which is still found in parts of Lancashire. Likewise, *clem* is a regionalism, a word meaning 'starve' in the Lancashire dialect, as is the grammatical construction *dunnot* for Standard English 'don't' or 'do not'. Other words such as *ay* for Standard English 'yes', and grammatical features, such as 'that there' and 'as' for Standard English 'who' or 'that' in 'Folk . . . as were either fools or not true men', are less regionally specific, but would certainly have been used by speakers of Lancashire dialect. The author here uses regionalisms sparingly but accurately to achieve the effect of contrasting Nicholas's speech with Margaret's without alienating the reader or making Nicholas seem unintelligent. On the contrary, his speech is very effective and his arguments both passionate and logical.

The three previous texts (Text 11, 12 and 13 on pp. 83, 85 and 86) are all examples of literary dialect, in which non-standard features, whether represented by semi-phonetic spelling, eye-dialect, allegro speech respellings or regionalisms, are employed sparingly by authors who otherwise write in

Standard English. Text 14: *Bite Bigger* is a verse from John Hartley's poem *Bite Bigger*. Hartley wrote poems in Yorkshire dialect for a Yorkshire readership, recited them at the Beacon Club in Halifax, and published them in the *Clock Almanac*, based in Wakefield. Poems, stories and recitations in local dialect became popular in the nineteenth century, when workers in industrial towns and cities, especially in the North of England, had enough leisure time to attend entertainments in music halls and mechanics' institutes, and were literate enough to read the relatively cheap publications produced locally. These texts were written by dialect speakers for dialect speakers, so the use of dialect features is much more dense: in this extract there are 31 words, if we count, e.g. 'th'moost', 'th'street' as single words, and 16 of these, or 51.6 per cent, have some dialectal feature.

Text 14: *Bite Bigger*

	Translation
Here's *a* apple, *an' th'mooast on* it's *saand*,	Here's an apple, and most of it's sound,
What's rotten *Aw'll* throw into *th'street*,	What's rotten I'll throw into the street,
Worn't it *gooid* to *lig thear* to be *faand*?	Wasn't it good to lie there to be found?
Nah booath on us *con* have a treat.	Now both of us can have a treat.

Commentary

Here, Hartley makes extensive use of both semi-phonetic spellings and regionalisms. The spellings <saand>, <faand> and <nah> for 'sound', 'found' and 'now' represent the use of /aː/ for RP /au/, a pronunciation still heard in some parts of Yorkshire today. <mooast> and <booath> for 'most' and 'both' suggest the pronunciation /ʊe/, while <gooid> for *good* represents the diphthong /ui/ and <thear> for 'there' /iə/. These pronunciations are much more regionally specific than those indicated in Texts 11, 12 and 13: indeed, they would be hard to interpret for anybody not already familiar with the accent. The reduced definite article <th'> appears here in <th'mooast> and <th'street>: although this would be more likely to be pronounced as /t/ or a glottal stop in present-day Yorkshire dialects, the /θ/ pronunciation was much more common in the nineteenth and early twentieth centuries. Other regionalisms here include the use of *on* where Standard English would have *of* in <th'mooast on it> and <booath on us>, and the word *lig* for Standard English 'lie'. The form <worn't> includes both regionalism, in that the verb is *were* rather than *was* and semi-phonetic spelling, in that <o> is used rather than <e> to suggest the Yorkshire pronunciation with /ɔː/. Hartley does use one allegro speech respelling, <an'> for Standard English 'and', but he does not use eye-dialect. The effect is to make this poem inaccessible to outsiders, but for that very reason, it is both humorous and 'homely' for the in-group (i.e. speakers of Yorkshire dialect) who share the dialect just as the father in the poem shares an apple with his son.

In Texts 11 to 14, we have seen how authors from the nineteenth to the late twentieth century have made use of semi-phonetic spelling, eye-dialect, allegro speech respellings and regionalisms to convey regional or, in the case of *Trainspotting*, national dialect. We have also noted the difference in density of dialect features between the literary dialect of the Texts 11 to 13, where the author provides enough 'clues' to give the reader a flavour of the dialect without making it inaccessible, and the dialect literature of Text 14, which is primarily intended for speakers of the dialect.

Activity

Using this framework, prepare some notes for a commentary on Text 15: *English Heretic*.

Internal aspects
• What semi-phonetic spellings are used in the text to indicate regional pronunciation?   • Is there any use of eye-dialect in this text?   • What regional vocabulary is used in the text (regionalisms)?   • What features of grammar in the text are regional or non-standard (regionalisms)?   • Are there any interesting features of graphology in this text?   • What is the density of dialect features in this text (as a percentage of total words)?
External aspects
• Who is writing the text?   • For what purpose are they writing the text?   • For what audience are they writing the text?   • What is the text's level of formality?   • What attitudes, values and assumptions are in the text?   • What kind of text are they producing?
All of the above form part of the *context* of the text.

(Adapted from *A Framework for Looking at Texts*, published by LINC in *Language in the National Curriculum*, p. 84)

Text 15: *English Heretic*

'Hey, Kenty, how old do 'ee think I are?'
so comes boy Ashley Trudgeon's claywork grammar,
then, 'She d'do more than 'er did do, dun't 'er?'
the crystal clear question asked by my father.

> In England, a boy I taught, joked to me
> that for the Cornish, a rake was technical.
> I laughed it off (as you do frequently),
> But inside hist'ry raged, went political.

I've long thought t'text the bugger back,
'n tell 'un of my degrees, my Ph.D.:
Yew boy: dun't U think we Cornish are slack.
They tried an' failed t'kick 'un out o'me.

> So please, to this English heretic drink.
> Our words are warmer that way I think.
> I'll write my homilies the way we d'speak:
> I *are* the poet: do 'ee at your language geek.

(Kent 2002: 41)

(There is commentary on p. 96.)

SUMMARY

In this unit, we have discussed the differences between dialect litera-ture, written entirely in dialect, and literary dialect, in which dialect is used for specific purposes within texts that are otherwise written in Standard English. The density of dialect features, in terms of overall percentage of words that differ in some way from the Standard, tends to be higher in dialect literature, which is often written for readers who know the dialect. We have discussed the devices used by authors to convey dialect: semi-phonetic spelling, eye-dialect, allegro speech respellings and regionalisms, and have examined the use of these devices by a range of authors from the nineteenth century to the present day.

We have also discussed the intended effects of the use of dialect in literature, from the humorous use of stereotyped features to the representation of dialect as the voice of a minority, to make a political point.

Extension

Try to 'translate' a well-known story, such as *Red Riding Hood*, or *The Three Bears* into your local dialect. What decisions do you need to make about the following:

- Use of semi-phonetic spelling. Should you use this throughout, or only on selected words where the regional pronunciation is very salient?

- Use of dialect vocabulary. Do you need to provide a glossary?

- Setting. Should you change the 'cottage in the woods' to a council flat, or a miners' cottage?

- Are you going to make the translation humorous or not?

There are several 'translator' websites in which you can enter text in Standard English and have it 'translated' into a dialect. Some of these can be found at www.whoohoo.co.uk but you can find others by typing the name of your dialect followed by 'translator' into a search engine. Try entering the Standard English text of your tale, and compare the result with your own translation.

commentaries

Unit two (Text 4), p. 28

In Text 4, (A) is the front of the T-shirt and (B) is the back. Unlike Text 3: Word for Northerners (p. 17), this presents us with isolated words (A) and their definitions (B) rather than continuous text. Some of these words are distinct **lexical items**, while others differ from the Standard (US) English version only in terms of the semi-phonetic spelling, which indicates a distinct pronunciation.

Some of the words reflect the fact that many of the earliest English-speaking settlers in Pittsburgh were of Ulster Scots (known in the US as 'Scotch-Irish') extraction. Their ancestors had previously migrated from Scotland to Northern Ireland, so some of the words found in Pittsburgh dialect are also used in Scotland and Northern Ireland today. Examples of such words are *jaggers*, *nebby*, *redd up* and *slippy*. *Jaggers* defined on the back of the T-shirt as 'thorns', is clearly related to the Scots use of *jag* for Standard English *jab* meaning 'injection': the *Dictionary of the Scots Language* (*DSL*) (www.dsl.ac.uk/dsl/) defines it as 'a prick'. *Nebby* meaning 'nosey', comes from the word *neb*, which, in Scotland and the North of England can mean a promontory (which juts out like a nose) or a nose. The *OED* has the following definition:

> 1. Interfering, inquisitive, nosy.
> *Sc. National Dict.* s.v. *nebbie*, records the sense in use across a broad swathe of Central and Southern Scotland in 1963. *Dict. Amer. Regional Eng.* s.v. records the sense as common chiefly in Pennsylvania.

In fact, *nebby* is also used in the North of England, but it must have been taken to Pittsburgh by the settlers from Northern Ireland.

Redd up meaning 'to tidy' is not marked as Scots or dialectal in the *OED Online*, but many of the citations given are from Scotland or the North of England. The *DSL* defines *To mak (ane) red* as: 'To make a clearance, to clear up (a disordered or untidy place)' and states that it is only found in Scotland and the North of England.

Slipp(e)y, meaning the same as Standard English *slippery*. The *OED Online* does not mark this word as Scots or dialectal, but *DSL* states that, apart from being in general use in Scotland, it is 'now only dial. in England'.

All four of these words are presented on the T-shirt as if they are exclusive to the Pittsburgh dialect. The fact that they have been so fully 'claimed' by Pittsburghers demonstrates the importance of the 'Scotch-Irish' heritage in this city. The word *babushka* shows the influence of another group of settlers, those who came from Eastern Europe in the late nineteenth and early twentieth centuries. Meaning 'a head scarf', it comes from the Russian word for 'granny'.

Gumban is defined as 'rubber band' ('elastic band' in British English). The German word for this is *Gummiband*, and, since the earliest settlers, along with the 'Scotch-Irish' were the Germans who have since become known as the Pennsylvania Dutch (from *Deutsch*, meaning 'German'), this word could be an example of their influence on 'Pittsburghese'.

Other words included here are not specifically from Scots or other European languages, but, within the US, are seen as peculiar to Pittsburgh. *Spicket* meaning 'a tap on a beer barrel' is a variant of Standard English *spigot* and is listed in the *OED* as 'US and dial.', while *DSL* cites it as Scots and also in English dialects. *Pop* for a 'carbonated soft drink' may seem unremarkable to British readers, but, within North America it is very marked as either Pittsburghese or Canadian usage. *Chitchat* is cited in the *OED Online* as having the same definition given in Text 4B, and, since it is not marked as dialectal in *OED* and not even listed in *DSL*, this must be a colloquial English word that has been retained in Pittsburgh.

Other words listed in Text 4B are peculiar to the Pittsburgh dialect because their **referents** are items or phenomena that are peculiar to Pittsburgh and/or have a special cultural resonance there. *Chipped Ham* is defined in Text 4B as 'thinly sliced ham sold only in the Burgh'; *Iron* is the local beer; *Jumbo* is a type of Bologna sausage; *the Burgh* is Pittsburgh itself; *the Mon* one of the rivers that run through the city and *the Point* 'the meeting place of Pittsburgh's three rivers'. The shortening of names in *the Burgh* and *the Mon* along with the use of the definite article to denote the fact that this is 'the one and only', is a feature used elsewhere to refer to a home town or city, such as 'The Pool' for Liverpool. *Blitzburgh* is a humorous nickname for the city, as can be seen from the definition 'a drinking town with a football problem'.

Most of the other words in Text 4B demonstrate the use of semi-phonetic spelling to indicate features of the Pittsburgh accent. In *aht, dahn-tahn*, we see the use of <ah> to indicate the pronunciation /aː/ for RP/General American /au/. *Gumban* and *hans* show the loss of /d/ at the end of a word and before plural –s, while *pensivania* shows the loss of /l/ before the /v/. *Picksburgh* shows the pronunciation of /t/ as /k/ which is found in a number of English accents in words such as *little* (childish 'ickle'). *Jeetjet? No, j'ew?* shows the way in which *did you* in rapid speech becomes pronounced as

/dʒ/, represented here as <j>: this is by no means peculiar to Pittsburgh, but would be a feature of rapid speech in many varieties of English. *Sammitch* for 'sandwich' likewise shows the kind of assimilation found in rapid speech: the /d/ is lost, then the /n/ becomes an /m/ because a /w/ follows (try saying 'sandwich' quickly, and you will find that your lips move together to make the /w/ before you have finished the /n/, so that it becomes /m/), finally, the /w/ is lost, giving us the pronunciation indicated here. *Stillers* (meaning the Pittsburgh Steelers football team) and *stillmill* indicate the shortening of /iː/ to /ɪ/ in *steel*. *Keller* for 'colour' shows the pronunciation of /ʌ/ as /ɛ/, and *worsh* indicates that the vowel in 'wash' is lengthened to /ɔː/. *Jynt Igle* for 'joint eagle' indicates the pronunciation of 'joint' with /ai/.

As the text consists of isolated words, there is not much to comment on under the heading of grammar. However, the word *yins* can be discussed here because it is a form of the second-person pronoun peculiar to Pittsburgh. The definition in Text 4B specifically refers to this form as differentiating the dialect of Pittsburgh from those to the East (including eastern Pennsylvania, New Jersey, New York), where *yous* performs the same function, and those to the South, where *y'all* is used. All these forms have arisen in these regional varieties to compensate for the lack of distinction between singular and plural *you* in Standard English. The form *yins* is so closely associated with Pittsburgh that its citizens are known as *Yinzers*.

The graphology of Text 4 is interesting. On the front of the T-shirt, the words appear in a variety of fonts and are placed at various angles, presumably to catch the eye. The word 'Pittsburghese' appears in large black letters with a gold outline, 'Pittsburgh, Pennsylvania' also in black with a gold outline appears at the bottom, and some of the 'jumbled' words are in gold. Black and gold are the colours of the Pittsburgh Steelers football team. On the front of the T-shirt, the words appear above a picture of the Pittsburgh skyline, indicating a close association between the city and its dialect. On the back of the T-shirt (B), 'Pittsburghese' again appears in black and gold capitals, then the words which appear on the front are listed in alphabetical order in bold, followed by an initial or abbreviation in italics indicating part of speech, and then the definition in a regular font. This is the standard 'dictionary' format with which any reader would be familiar. The use of this layout on the back of the T-shirt gives the impression that 'Pittsburghese' is a 'language' that needs to be translated for strangers, even though, as we have seen, many of the 'words' are just phonetic variants of words found in Standard English/General American.

If we now move on to consider the external aspects of Text 4, the first thing to note is that the author is unknown. Like Text 3, this is one of a series of texts in 'Pittsburghese' that can be found on websites, on post-cards and in booklets. The words and definitions are taken from one to another and, in this case, there is no claim for copyright on the part of the author. What we do know is that he or she produced this text in order to print it on a T-shirt that would then be sold to tourists. As such, this represents an interesting development, the commodification of dialect as a resource for the tourist industry. The genre of the text is one that we also see represented in booklet form: the humorous dialect dictionary. The use of semi-phonetic spelling in, e.g. <dahntahn> exaggerates the distinctiveness of the dialect, and the layout in Text 4B parodies that of a 'serious' dictionary. The attitudes, values and assumptions behind this text are rather complex: on the one hand, it could be seen as poking gentle fun at the city and its dialect, but on the other hand, it includes statements that demonstrate affection for, and pride in, the city. 'The burgh' is 'a helluva cool place', 'pensivania' is 'the state where friends and memories last a lifetime'. The city's 'blue-collar' heritage as the foremost producer of steel in the US is celebrated in references to the industry ('stillmill') and to the stereotypical male, working-class pursuits of drinking and football (references to the local brew 'Iron' and the 'Stillers'). Like Text 3, Text 4 both celebrates and makes gentle fun of the city and its dialect by using a combination of formal and informal usage.

Unit six (Text 9), p. 75

One feature of non-standard grammar that both these extracts contain is the double negative. A has *he never worked no more*, while B has *I'm not harmed nowt* and *she couldn't get no buses*. As we have seen, double negatives are used in most, if not all, regional dialects of English. Some recent studies (Cheshire, Edwards and Whittle (1993) and Anderwald (2002)) have suggested that they are used less frequently in Northern English dialects than in Southern ones, but, as the extracts here show, they do occur in both Tyneside and Sheffield.

Another feature that the two extracts have in common is a tendency for plural nouns not to have the -*s* ending when there is a number before them. This is found in a number of non-standard dialects and, in some cases, even in Standard English, in the phrase *five foot two*. The construction is perfectly logical: the number tells us that the noun is plural, so why mark it again with -*s*? A has two instances of this: *eighteen or nineteen year* and *He was in the hospital for six month*, while B has *up to this last thirty year*. However, when the word *year* does not have a number before it, in *all these years*, it does take the -*s*.

Both speakers use the form *come* as the past tense form of the verb *to come*. A says *then I come ower here*, while B says of her parents, both of whom are dead *My mother come from Walkley and my dad come from Huddersfield*.

B the uses *come* in the perfect tense in *I've come to live down here*. This levelling of verb forms, where tenses that are marked by distinct forms in Standard English have the same form, is very common in many dialects of English. Other examples are *done* for Standard English *did*, as in *The boy done good*, and *seen* for *saw* in *I seen that last night*.

The two extracts show a very clear contrast in the use of the definite article. A uses the full form of the article *the*, whereas B never uses this. She either reduces the article to what is spelt here as <t'>, but is pronounced as a glottal stop, as in *he worked in t'brickyard*, or doesn't use it at all, as in *other one; in rolling mill;* and *in steel works*. This feature is known as definite article reduction: the article may be pronounced as a glottal stop, as /t/, more rarely as /θ/, or may be missed out completely. Definite article reduction is still very common in parts of Lancashire, Greater Manchester and Yorkshire. The comedian Peter Kay has popularised this feature with his use of the phrase *on t'internet*.

Not only does A always use the full form of *the*, she uses it where speakers of Standard English and many other regional dialects would not, in *He was in the hospital* and *Jimmy was only about the twenty-two*. In the first example, she is telling us not that her father was in a specific hospital, but that he was hospitalised: in this case, I would certainly say *he was in hospital*. The second example is more striking – to use *the* before a number is very unusual, but this speaker does this elsewhere in the interview, so it can't be a mistake.

Another feature used by A but not B is the personal pronoun *wor*: *wor Thomas* and *wor little Steven*. Here, *wor* is equivalent to Standard English *our* and is one of a number of personal pronouns that have a different form in Tyneside English. However, a Standard English speaker would probably not use *our* in this context, i.e. referring to her sons, but would simply say *Thomas* and *little Steven*. The use of *our* or *wor* before the names of relatives is typical of Northern English dialects, where a wife or girlfriend will be referred to as *our lass* and a brother (usually a younger brother, rarely a sister) as *our kid*.

A uses the form *divn't* in the phrase *I divn't know*. This is typical of Tyneside English, and not found in England outside the North East. Although there are no examples in the earlier extract, B says *don't know* elsewhere in her interview.

A uses the form *for to* before an **infinitive** verb in *That was for me for to get bread in for the bairns* (*bairns* = 'children'). In Standard English, only *to* would be used before an infinitive. The *for to* construction was common in earlier English, but is now found only in dialects, such as those of Scotland and parts of the North of England. It is not used by B, but Shorrocks (1999) found it in his interviews with speakers from Bolton.

Moving on to consider the features peculiar to B, one that is more common in Yorkshire than in Tyneside is the use of *were* in the third-person singular as in *when strike were on*. In Yorkshire, broad dialect speakers tend to use *were* in all persons (*I were, you were, she were, we were, they were*), whereas in Tyneside, it is more usual to find *was* throughout (*you was, we was, they was*).

In the phrase *all news what's going off*, B uses *what* as a **relative marker**. In Standard English *that* or *which* would be used in this context. *What* is very common in many dialects of English and Cheshire, Edwards and Whittle (1993) suggest that it is spreading throughout Britain. However, Beal and Corrigan (2005), comparing a larger number of speakers from Tyneside and Sheffield, found that, while this was very common in Sheffield, it was much rarer in the speech of Tynesiders.

Finally, one feature of B's speech that you might not have considered a matter of grammar is her tendency to use the word *love* as in *Well both lads have got made redundant, love* and *slogging hard love*. *Love* is a term of endearment used here by an older woman to a younger woman, and it seems to be used as a **discourse marker** when B wants to emphasise the importance of what she has said. These terms of endearment are very common in regional dialects, and are quite distinctive. In Sheffield and much of the North, *love* is used, in Derbyshire and Nottinghamshire *duck*, in Lancashire *chuck* or *cock*, in the West Midlands *chick*, in Glasgow *doll* or *hen* and in the North East of England a whole raft of terms are used including *pet*, *hinny* and *bonny lad*. Because most of these words tend to be used by men to address women, or by older speakers to address younger speakers, they have been the subject of much controversy as they are perceived as patronising or sexist. There have been newspaper stories of Northern call-centre workers being instructed not to use such terms to customers. However, the use of these terms is more complicated: in Sheffield and Leeds, working-class (apparently heterosexual) men, commonly address each other as *love*: in this context, it means nothing more or less than *mate*, a word that can be friendly, patronising or even threatening, depending on the context. The problem is that all these terms imply a familiarity that can be positive or negative, depending on the circumstances.

Unit seven (Text 15), p. 89

Looking first at the internal aspects of Text 15: *English Heretic*, there are a few instances of semi-phonetic spelling. In the first and last lines <'ee> represents the non-standard pronoun *ye*, but the apostrophe indicates that the initial /j/ is not pronounced. In South Western dialects of English, it is common for both /j/ and /w/ to be deleted at the beginning of words such as *year*, *woman* and, conversely, for them to be added to the beginning of works such as *earth*, *oats*. Initial /h/ is not pronounced in *her*, which is here spelt <'er> in line 2. The spelling <yew> for *you* in line 11 could be classed as semi-phonetic, as it may indicate a diphthong /iu/ rather than the 'pure' vowel /juː/, but such pronunciations are so widespread that this may simply be **eye-dialect**.

Allegro speech respelling is used in several places: *and* is spelt <'n> in line 9 and <an'> in line 12, suggesting the pronunciations /n̩/ and /an/, both of which are possible in speech, while <o'me> in line 12 and <hist'ry> in line 8 show deletion of the consonant from *of* and the <o> from *history*, both of which are common in colloquial English. The spellings <t'text> and <d'speak> indicate that the vowels of *to* and *do* are not pronounced. These could be classified as semi-phonetic spellings rather than allegro speech respellings, since the elision of the vowel in cases like this is not as widespread as, say, the loss of the first syllable in <'cos> for *because*.

There are a number of regionalisms in Text 15, but hardly any of these involve regional vocabulary. The only non-standard word in the poem is *geek*: according to Wright's *The English Dialect Dictionary*, this word is only found in Cornwall, where it means 'to look, stare intently or gaze'. (The noun *geek* as in 'computer geek' is a different word.) So here the poet is telling those who criticise his dialect to look at their own language. The word *claywork* in line 2 is not dialectal, but it does refer to the Cornish china clay industry: the boy's grammar is as much part of Cornwall as the clay that comes from the county's earth. The proper noun *Kenty* in the first line is likewise not dialectal, but colloquial, as the use of a surname plus the suffix *-y* is a familiar form of address in most dialects of British English, especially between males. Likewise, the *bugger*, used in line 9, is a mild swear word used throughout Britain.

The poet makes much greater use of regional grammar: many of the semi-phonetic spellings that we have already commented on are also grammatical regionalisms. The pronouns are very different from those of Standard English: <'ee> where Standard English would have *you*; <'er> for SE *she* and <'un> for SE *him*. These are all found in dialects of the South West of England: <'ee> is a semi-phonetic spelling of *ye* or perhaps *thee*, both of which were found in earlier English and are preserved in dialects; <'un> has not been analysed as semi-phonetic spelling, because it is not a pronunciation of *him*, but a totally different form, sometimes spelt <'en> in this dialect. It may be a relic of the Old English form *hine*. The form <'er> is a semi-phonetic spelling of *her*, but in this context ('er did do), where it is the **subject** of the sentence, Standard English would have *she*. This is an example of pronoun exchange, a feature of South Western dialects where what would be the subject and object pronouns in Standard English 'swap' places. So Standard English 'She said to me' would be 'Her said to I'.

<Dun't> for *doesn't* has not been analysed as semi-phonetic spelling because the spelling represents not just a different pronunciation, but a difference in **morphology** between the dialect represented here and Standard English. In SE, *doesn't* has contraction of the negative *not* to -*n't*, but this dialect, like some Northern ones, has a secondary contraction, where the <s> of the verb is also lost.

Another regionalism that is very prominent in this poem is the use of the verb *do* in various forms before other verbs. In Standard English, this can only happen when *do* is used for emphasis (see Unit six), but in South Western dialects *do* is used in non-emphatic contexts. That *do* is not emphatic, except in the last line, is indicated by the elision of the vowel in the semi-phonetic spelling <d'do>. The repetition of *do* in the quoted speech in line 3 may look strange to speakers of SE or other dialects, but its meaning is 'crystal clear'. In fact, this use of *do* was common in Standard English until about 1700, and is preserved in dialects of the South West of England, as well as Welsh and Irish Englishes.

In the first and last lines, *are* is used where Standard English would have *am*. In regional dialects, forms of the verb 'to be' are very often different from the Standard English pattern. Hughes, Trudgill and Watt point this out:

> Forms of the verb *to be*, particularly in the present tense, show much greater variation in Traditional Dialects than in more modern forms of speech. . . . In parts of the West Midlands, *am* may be generalized to all persons, as in *you am*, while in areas of the south-west, *be* may be generalized to all persons of the verb – that is, *you be, he be*, etc.
>
> (2005: 34–5)

In this case, the Cornish dialect has *are* in both the singular ('I are') and the plural ('we Cornish are').

The poem uses graphology for contrast, with italics used to emphasise the use of dialect in direct speech. Lines 1, 11 and 12 are entirely in italics, representing the words addressed to the poet by Ashley Trudgeon and the poet's planned text message to the schoolboy who insulted him. In the last line, the words *are* and *do* are also in italics, both to show that they would be strongly stressed in speech, and because, as we have discussed, they are features of dialect grammar that stand out as very different from Standard English. In line 11, 'you' is spelt both <yew> and <U>: the first of these is, as we have discussed, an example of semi-phonetic spelling, but the <U> is exactly how this word would be spelt in a text message. Here, the poet is writing what he would like to 'text the bugger back'.

If we count items such as *t'kick, d'speak* as single words, there are 130 words in this poem, of which 22 have some dialectal feature, giving a density of 17 per cent. This is a little higher than the density of dialect in the extract from *Trainspotting* (14 per cent), but much lower than that of *Bite Bigger* (51 per cent), so we would class this as literary dialect rather than dialect literature. However, the measure of density is somewhat misleading here, as the poem has some lines that are entirely in Standard English, and others that are much denser with dialect features. Take lines 2 and 3:

> then, 'She d'do more than 'er did do, dun't 'er?'
> the crystal clear question asked by my father.

Line 2 has five out of ten words with some dialect feature, so has a 50 per cent density, while line 3 has none, so a zero per cent density. The reason for this is that the poet is representing, on the one hand, the different voices of his father, Ashley Trudgeon and the 'English' boy, and, on the other hand, the different **codes** that he, as a poet and a Cornishman, uses in everyday life.

This brings us neatly to the external features of the poem. The poet, Alan M. Kent, was, according to the biography in the volume from which this poem was taken, 'born in the china-clay mining region in mid-Cornwall and . . . educated at the universities of Cardiff and Exeter, gaining a doctorate in Cornish and Anglo-Cornish Literature. He . . . has written extensively on the literary and cultural history of Cornwall' (Kent 2004: 212). As well as Standard English and the dialect of English spoken in Cornwall, now known as Cornu-English, Kent also speaks Cornish, which is not a dialect of English but a completely separate Celtic language, related to Welsh and Breton. The 'switching' from Standard to Cornu-English that we have observed in our analysis of the poem, would be completely natural to a highly educated Cornishman such as Alan M. Kent.

The poem is written in English because a poem in Cornish would not have a wide readership, but also because it addresses the relationship between Cornwall and 'England'. Although Cornwall is officially a county of England, many Cornish people have a very strong sense that they have a separate identity, and that Cornwall constitutes a nation. The revival of the Cornish language in the twentieth century was one expression of this identity: textbooks will tell you that Cornish 'died' in the eighteenth century, but Alan M. Kent and others are now native speakers. However, there are many more people in Cornwall who have just as strong a sense of Cornish identity, but have not had the opportunity to learn Cornish: for them, and for bilinguals, Cornu-English, the dialect used in this poem, expresses that identity. Other symbols of Cornish identity include the use of the flag with St Piran's cross (white on a black background): you can see this on car stickers, souvenirs and on the packaging of Ginster's pies and pasties (the pasty being a traditional Cornish food). Groups such as Tyr-Gwyr-Gweryn (Cornish for 'Land-Truth-People') lobby for recognition of this separate identity. Their website has a substantial entry on 'the Cornish Nation', which begins as follows:

> It is abundantly clear that given the official attitudes to the Cornish people over many years that there will be an almost insurmountable wall to climb over in getting the State and its puppets to have the honesty and integrity to recognise the existence of the Cornish nation.
>
> (www.kernowtgg.co.uk)

The attitudes, values and assumptions behind this quotation are very much tied in with the poet's attitude to Cornishness. The poem addresses issues of Cornish identity both in terms of what is said, and the dialect used. Kent sets up an opposition between 'England' and Cornwall, by telling us that it was 'in England' that the schoolboy told him the joke about Cornish technology that, though shrugged off at the time, angered him and provoked him to write this poem 'inside hist'ry raged, went political'. The 'joke' refers to the same stereotypes of the Cornish and other rural groups that were discussed in Unit three: they are considered to be technologically backward 'peasants' and their dialect is likewise perceived as 'unintelligent'. This is why the poet wants to 'text the bugger back' with news of his educational achievements, and why he points out that the dialect words of his father, quoted in line 3, are 'crystal clear'. The same point was made by William Labov in his paper 'The Logic of Non-standard English' (1972b), in which he analyses the speech of an African American Vernacular English (AAVE) speaker with that of a middle-class speaker of Standard American English. Labov concludes that, although the AAVE speaker uses constructions that would at that time have been condemned in the classroom, the logic of his argument is much clearer than that of the grammatically correct but 'waffly' middle-class speaker.

The poet's purpose in writing Text 15 is political. In this case 'the medium is the message', the poet asserts his identity by the act of writing in dialect: 'I *are* the poet'. The intended audience is the reasonably intelligent English reader who may be encouraged to re-examine his or her attitude to Cornwall: many liberal, well-intentioned people who would not dream of telling a racist or sexist joke may not have considered the joke about the rake 'politically incorrect' to the same degree, but this poem tells us that we should do. It would also be addressed to Cornish readers who would empathise with the poet.

The poem has several levels of formality, from the very informal direct speech in Cornu-English, to the more formal Standard English of the invitation to the reader in lines 13 and 14:

So please, to this English heretic drink.
Our words are warmer that way I think.

The informality of some of the language draws attention away from the fact that this is a poem with a regular rhyme scheme of ABAB, though the fact that many of the rhymes are on unstressed syllables (are/'er; grammar/father) makes this less obtrusive. The rhyme pattern changes to AABB in the final verse, the change drawing attention to these concluding lines in which the poet makes his point forcefully.

Text 15 is an excellent example of literary dialect being used to make a political point about language, identity and nationhood. These issues are addressed directly in the content of this poem, but, in a society where Standard English is the expected norm for printed texts, and, as we saw in Unit three, dialects are often associated with negative stereotypes, any use of dialect in literature is a political statement in itself.

phonetic symbols

Throughout this book, I have used phonetic symbols to denote sounds, because, as we have seen in Units two and seven, semi-phonetic spelling is imprecise, and often depends on the reader having prior knowledge of the dialect referred to. Once you have learned the International Phonetic Alphabet (IPA), you will be able to refer to any sound used in any language, and recognise any sound denoted in this alphabet, at least with a copy of the IPA to hand. I have also used keywords, written in capitals, to refer to vowel and diphthong sounds used in sets of words, for example BATH. These were devised by Wells (1982), and have been generally adopted by linguists as a useful way of comparing pronunciations in different accents of English. These keywords are used in the following table, and, unless stated otherwise, the phonetic symbols refer to the pronunciation in modern RP. Sometimes an IPA symbol appears more than once with different keywords because the sets of words are pronounced differently in other accents: for instance, Northern English accents have /aː/ in START but not in BATH.

IPA Symbol	Keyword	Examples
/ɪ/	KIT	*ship, sick, bridge, milk, myth, busy*
/ɛ/	DRESS	*step, neck, edge, shelf, friend, ready*
/a/	TRAP	*tap, back, badge, scalp, hand, cancel*
/ɒ/	LOT	*stop, sock, dodge, romp, possible, quality*
/ʌ/	STRUT	*cup, suck, budge, pulse, trunk, blood*
/ʊ/	FOOT	*put, push, full, good, look, wolf*
/ɑː/	BATH	*staff, brass, ask, dance, sample, calf*
/ɒ/	CLOTH	*cough, broth, cross, long, Boston*
/əː/	NURSE	*hurt, lurk, urge, burst, jerk, term*
/iː/	FLEECE	*creep, speak, leave, feel, key, people*
/eɪ/	FACE	*tape, cake, raid, veil, steak, day*
/ɑː/	PALM	*psalm, father, bra, spa, lager*
/ɔː/	THOUGHT	*taught, sauce, hawk, jaw, broad*
/əʊ/	GOAT	*soap, joke, home, know, so, roll*
/uː/	GOOSE	*loop, shoot, tomb, mute, huge, view*
/aɪ/	PRICE	*ripe, write, arrive, high, try, buy*

/ɔɪ/	CHOICE	*adroit, noise, join, toy, royal*
/aʊ/	MOUTH	*out, house, loud, count, crowd, crow*
/ɪə/	NEAR	*beer, sincere, fear, beard, serum*
/ɛə/	SQUARE	*care, fair, pear, where, scarce, vary*
/ɑː/	START	*far, sharp, bark, carve, farm, heart*
/ɔː/	NORTH	*for, war, short, scorch, born, warm*
/ɔː/	FORCE	*four, wore, sport, porch, borne, story*
/ʊə/	CURE	*poor, tourist, pure, plural, jury*
/ə/	*lett*ER	*better, paper, teacher, metre, sugar, anchor*

Consonants are usually represented by the phonetic symbol that corresponds most closely to the letter usually written for that sound, for instance, /n/ for <n> in *never*. Some sounds in English have no single letter to represent them, so I list the IPA symbols for these below:

/j/   as in YES, also used for the sound before /u/ in, e.g. *cute, beauty*. This sound is referred to as yod.

/ŋ/   as in SING, referred to as the velar nasal.

/n̩/   This is referred to as syllabic 'n', and represents the sound used when /n/ takes up the whole syllable, usually when a vowel would come before it in more 'careful' speech as in /sɛvn̩/ rather than /sɛvən/ for *seven*.

/ʃ/   as in SHIP.

/ʒ/   as in LEISURE.

/ʔ/   often used for /t/ but also for /p/, /k/ in some accents. This is referred to as the glottal stop.

/θ/   as in THIN.

/ð/   as in THIS.

/dʒ/   as in JOHN, GIN.

references and further reading

Abercrombie, D. (1951) 'R.P. and local accent' reprinted in 1965 in *Studies in Phonetics and Linguistics* London: Oxford University Press, pp. 10–15.

Anderwald, L. (2002) *Negation in Non-standard British English*. London: Routledge.

Beal, J.C. (2005) 'Dialect representations in texts' in Brown, K. (ed.) *The Encyclopedia of Language and Linguistics*, 2nd edition. Oxford: Elsevier, pp. 531–538.

Beal, J.C. and Corrigan, K.P. (2005) 'A tale of two dialects: relativisation in Newcastle and Sheffield' in Filppula, M., Palander, M., Klemola, J. and Penttilä, E. (eds) *Dialects across Borders*. Amsterdam: Benjamins, pp. 211–229.

Burbano-Elizondo, L. (2001) 'Lexical erosion and lexical innovation in Tyne and Wear', unpublished M.Litt. dissertation, Department of English Linguistic and Literary Studies, University of Newcastle upon Tyne.

Campbell, G. (1776) *The Philosophy of Rhetoric*. Edinburgh.

Chambers, J. and Trudgill, P. (1998) *Dialectology*. Cambridge: Cambridge University Press.

Cheshire, J., Edwards, V. and Whittle, P. (1993) 'Non-standard English and dialect levelling' in Milroy, J. and Milroy, L. (eds) *Real English: the Grammar of English Dialects in the British Isles*. London: Longman, pp. 53–96.

Cheshire, J. and Milroy, M. (1993) 'Syntactic variation in non-standard dialects: background issues' in Milroy, J. and Milroy, L. (eds) (1993) *Real English: the Grammar of English Dialects in the British Isles*. London: Longman, pp. 3–33.

Coleman, J. (2004) *A History of Cant and Slang Dictionaries*, Vol. 1: 1567–1784. Oxford: Oxford University Press.

Council for the Protection of Rural England, (2003) *The Lie of the Land*. London: CPRE.

Coupland, N. (1992) *Dialect in Use*. Clevedon: Multilingual Matters.

Crystal, D. (2003) *A Dictionary of Linguistics and Phonetics*, 5th edition. Oxford: Blackwell.

Edwards, J.R. (1979) *Language and Disadvantage*. London: Edward Arnold.

Foulkes, P. and Docherty, G. (eds) (1999) *Urban Voices: accent studies in the British Isles*. London: Arnold.

Freeborn, D. (1998) *From Old English to Standard English: a course book in language variation across time*. Basingstoke: Macmillan.

Giles, H. (1970) 'Evaluative reactions to accents' *Educational Review* 22: 211–227.

Giles, H. and Powesland, P.F. (1975) *Speech Style and Social Evaluation*. London: Academic.

Gimson, A.C. (1962) *An Introduction to the Pronunciation of English*. London: Arnold.

Greenwood, James (1711) *An Essay Towards a Practical English Grammar*. London: R. Tookey.

Hughes, A., Trudgill, P. and Watt, D. (2005) *English Accents and Dialects*, 4th edition. London: Arnold.

Johnstone, B. and Baumgardt, D. (2004) '"Pittsburghese" online: vernacular norming in conversation' *American Speech* 79: 115–145.

Kent, A.M. (2002) *The Hensbarrow Homilies*. Penzance: Patten Press.

Kent, A.M. (2004) *The Dreamt Sea: an anthology of Anglo-Cornish poetry 1928–2004*. London: Francis Boutle.

Kortmann, B. (ed.) (2004) *A Handbook of Varieties of English*. Berlin: Mouton.

Labov, W. (1972a) 'Subjective dimensions of a linguistic change in progress' in *Sociolinguistic Patterns*. Oxford: Basil Blackwell, pp. 143–159.

Labov, W. (1972b) 'The logic of non-standard English' in *Language in the Inner City: Studies in the Black English Vernacular*. Philadelphia: University of Pennsylvania Press, pp. 201–240.

Lambert, W.E., Frankel, H. and Tucker, R.A. (1966) 'Judging personality through speech: a French-Canadian example' *Journal of Communication* 16: 304–321.

Lambert, W.E., Hodgson, R.C., Gardner, R.D. and Fillenbaum, S. (1960) 'Evaluational reactions to spoken languages' *Journal of Abnormal and Social Psychology* 60: 44–51.

LINC (1992) *A Framework for Looking at Texts* in *Language in the National Curriculum: materials for professional development*. Nottingham: LINC, p. 84.

Llamas, C. (1999) 'A new methodology: data elicitation for social and regional language variation studies' *Leeds Working Papers in Linguistics* 7: 95–119.

Llamas, C. (2000) 'Middlesbrough English: convergent and divergent trends in a "Part of Britain with no identity"' *Leeds Working Papers in Linguistics* 8: 123–148.

McDonald, Christine (1980) 'Some contrasts in teachers' and pupils' language and aspects of their relevance in the classroom'. Unpublished dissertation, University of Newcastle.

McDonald, Christine (1981) 'Variation in the use of modal verbs with special reference to Tyneside English'. University of Newcastle Ph.D. thesis.

Milroy, J. and Milroy, L. (eds) (1993) *Real English: the grammar of English dialects in the British Isles*. London: Longman.

Opie, I. and Opie, P. (1959) *The Lore and Language of Schoolchildren*. Oxford: Oxford University Press.

Orton, H. and various others (1962 onwards) *Survey of English Dialects*. London: E.J. Arnold.

Orton, H., Sanderson, S. and Widdowson, J. (1978) *The Linguistic Atlas of England*. London: Croom Helm.

Orton, H. and Wright, N. (1974) *A Word Geography of England*. London: Seminar Press.

Petyt, K.M. (1985) *Dialect and Accent in Industrial West Yorkshire*. Amsterdam: Benjamins.

Shorrocks, G. (1999) *A Grammar of the Dialect of the Bolton Area*. Frankfurt: Peter Lang.

Strongman, K.T. and Woosley, J. (1967) 'Stereotypical reactions to regional accents' *British Journal of Social and Clinical Psychology* 6: 164–167.

Trudgill, P. (1974) *The Social Differentiation of English in Norwich*. Cambridge: Cambridge University Press.

Trudgill, P. (1983) *On Dialect*. Oxford: Basil Blackwell.

Trudgill, P. (ed.) (1984) *Language in the British Isles*. Cambridge: Cambridge University Press.

Trudgill, P. (1999) *The Dialects of England*, second edition. Oxford: Blackwell.

Trudgill, P. and Chambers, J. (1991) *Dialects of English: studies in grammatical variation*. London: Longman.

Upton, C., Parry, D. and Widdowson, J.D.A. (1994) *The Survey of English Dialects: the Dictionary and Grammar*. London: Routledge.

Upton, C., Sanderson, S. and Widdowson, J. (1987) *Word Maps: a dialect atlas of England*. London: Croom Helm.

Upton, C. and Widdowson, J.D.A. (1996) *An Atlas of English Dialects*. Oxford: Oxford University Press.

Walker, J. (1791) *A Critical Pronouncing Dictionary*. London: G.G.J. and J. Robinson and T. Cadell.

Wells, J.C. (1982) *Accents of English*. Cambridge: Cambridge University Press.

Welsh, I. (2004) *Trainspotting*. London: Random House.

Wright, J. (ed.) (1895–1905) *The English Dialect Dictionary*. Oxford: Oxford University Press.

Wright, J. (1905) *The English Dialect Grammar*. Oxford: Oxford University Press.

WEB-BASED RESOURCES

BBC Voices www.bbc.co.uk/voices/

Common Ground (a charity dedicated to preserving and promoting local distinctiveness) www.commonground.org.uk

Council for the Protection of Rural England www.cpre.org.uk

Peter Davidson's homepage (map of English regions) www.padav.demon.co.uk/englishregions.htm

Dialect Translators (Brummie, Geordie, Scouse, etc.) www.whoohoo.co.uk/main.asp

Dictionary of the Scots Language www.dsl.ac.uk/dsl/

Guardian Unlimited (to access articles from the *Guardian* and the *Observer*) www.guardian.co.uk

Leeds Working Papers in Linguistics
www.leeds.ac.uk/linguistics/research/research.htm

Newcastle Electronic Corpus of Tyneside English (NECTE) www.ncl.ac.uk/necte

Office of the Deputy Prime Minister (regional government) www.odpm.gov.uk

Oxford English Dictionary Online www.oed.com

Pittsburgh Speech and Society www.english.cmu.edu/pittsburghspeech/

Tyr-Gwyr-Gweryn (Cornish Nation) www.kernowtgg.co.uk

UK technical support (Word for Northerners) www.uktfs.co.uk

Urban Dictionary www.urbandictionary.com

Words (poetry texts) www.whitewolf.newcastle.edu.au/words

Yorkshire Dialect www.yorksj.ac.uk/dialect/

index of terms

Here, I provide brief definitions of those words that appear in bold type the first time they are used in this book. This is not meant to be a complete glossary of linguistic terms: for this, I would recommend Crystal (2003).

accent 9
A distinct (social or regional) type of pronunciation.

accommodation 31
This refers to the tendency for speakers to modify their speech to make it more similar to that of other people, usually those they admire or wish to impress.

active vocabulary 55
The set of words that a speaker uses, as opposed to those he or she knows or recognises.

adjective 71
A part of speech which modifies or refers to the quality of a noun or noun **phrase**, e.g. a *fast* car, your room is *untidy*.

adverb 71
A part of speech which modifies a verb, e.g. that car goes *fast/quickly*, you write *untidily*.

allegro speech respelling 84
A type of spelling used in **dialect** literature/literary dialect to represent the way words tend to be shortened when we speak quickly, such as <an'> for *and*.

allophone 49
A distinct pronunciation that, unlike a **phoneme**, cannot distinguish one word from another. Allophones can be predicted from the environment, such as the dark/clear /l/ in *hill/hilly*. Allophones are enclosed by square brackets, thus [ɫ], [l] are allophones of the phoneme /l/.

auxiliary verb 69
A verb that is used before a lexical verb in English to form negatives, **interrogatives** and various tenses such as perfect, future, or to avoid repeating a lexical verb. Auxiliaries include *be, can, do, have, may, might, must, shall* and *will*.

broad 11
(of **accents**) More extreme, showing a greater degree of difference from Standard English/**Received Pronunciation** (RP) or another prestigious variety.

clause 69
A unit that is shorter than a sentence, but contains a verb. 'When I called, you were busy', is one sentence, but two clauses.

clear 49

With reference to /l/, the clear **allophone** is the more consonantal one heard in RP *hilly*.

code 99

One of the varieties in a speaker's linguistic repertoire. This can be a language or a **dialect**. Code-switching is what happens when a speaker 'switches' from regional dialect to standard, or, for instance, from Welsh to English, in the course of a conversation.

colloquialism 61

A word that is widely used in informal speech or writing, and not regionally, though it may be nationally, restricted. For example *bloke* is a colloquial word for *man* in Britain and Australia, but not in North America.

comparative 71

A form of the **adjective** or **adverb** that compares the degree of a quality of two nouns or verbs, such as *fitter/more healthy*; *faster/more speedily*.

consonant 9

A sound that involves either closure or constriction of the flow of air through the mouth and/or nose.

contraction 79

In English, this involves shortening one form and attaching it to the form before it, so *has not* becomes *hasn't*.

convergence 9

In speech accommodation, this is the process of altering your speech to be more similar to that of another person.

dark 49

The **allophone** of /l/ in English, which is more 'vowel-like'. In RP, this is found after a vowel and before a **consonant** or at the end of a word, as in *hill*, *hilt*.

definite article 69

A word used with a noun, where the referent (thing, person, etc. referred to by the noun) is something or somebody specific. When we say or write *The book on the table is mine* we have a specific book in mind.

dialect 1

A distinct (social or regional) variety in which grammar and vocabulary as well as pronunciation are different from those of other dialects.

diphthong 43

A vowel sound in which there is a change from one vowel to another within the same syllable.

discourse marker 96

A word or **phrase** used in conversation not so much for its literal meaning as to signal the speaker's attitude, changes in topic, turn-taking, etc. An example is *like* in 'She's, like, so not going out with him'.

divergence 9

In speech accommodation this is the process of altering your speech to be more different from that of another person.

Estuary English 15

A term used to describe a variety of English said to be spreading from London and the Thames Estuary throughout the South East of England and beyond, including features such as **glottalisation**, labial /r/ and 'th-fronting'.

eye-dialect 23

A device used in **dialect** literature and literary dialect when the author wishes to give an impression of non-standard and/or uneducated speech. The form represents a pronunciation that would be common in most **accents**, including RP, but that gives an impression of uneducated usage because of deviant spelling. An example is <wot> for *what*.

genre 25

A particular style of writing, usually associated with a specific style.

glottalisation 9

The process in which a **consonant** is formed by closing or narrowing the glottis, which is the opening between the vocal chords. If the glottis is completely closed and then released, the result is a glottal stop [ʔ], but if it is narrowed, and the air is released through another part of the vocal tract, as for /p/, /t/, or /k/, the consonant is glottalised /ʔp/, /ʔt/, /ʔk/.

grammatical gender 72

A system of classifying nouns whereby their agreement with **adjectives**, articles, etc. has no correspondence with natural categories of male/female, animate/inanimate, etc. French, German and many other European languages have grammatical gender, so that *la table* (the table) is 'feminine'; *das Mädchen* (the girl) is neuter.

graphology 16

This refers to the spelling, punctuation and design of a text.

infinitive 95

The base form of the verb, without any endings for **tense** or **person**. In English, this can either appear with *to* as in *I like to dance* or without, as in *I can dance*.

interrogative 69

The form used when a question is asked.

jargon 25

A set of words used by a sub-section of society, such as a profession or interest group.

lexical attrition 55

The loss of words from the vocabulary of a particular language or **dialect**.

lexical item 91

An individual word in the sense of a separate dictionary item, rather than an alternative spelling of a word.

lexis 53

The linguistic term for vocabulary.

macdonaldisation 4

A term used to describe the process whereby products are standardised (as in fast food chains) and so shops, etc. look exactly the same in every town.

matched guise 30

A type of linguistic experiment intended to elicit attitudes to languages or **dialects** in which participants are asked to judge samples of speech that they are

113

led to believe have been produced by different speakers, but that have in fact all been performed by the same speaker.

mild   33

(of **accents**) Less extreme, showing a lesser degree of difference from Standard English/RP or another prestigious variety.

modal   69

In English, a set of auxiliary verbs that express attitudes such as uncertainty, necessity, possibility, etc. as well as futurity. Like other **auxiliaries**, they have the NICE properties. The modal verbs in English are *can*, *could*, *may*, *might*, *must*, *shall*, *should*, *will* and *would*. *Dare*, *need* and *ought* are semi-modals because the do not always exhibit the NICE properties: *dare* can have either *daren't* or *don't dare* in the negative, for instance.

monophthong   43

A vowel sound that does not involve any change of articulation within a syllable.

morphology   98

The part of grammar that deals with the structure of words. Inflectional morphology deals with the way morphemes are added to mark tense in verbs, number in nouns, etc., while derivational morphology deals with the way morphemes are added to create new words.

natural gender   72

A system of classifying nouns whereby their agreement with **adjectives**, articles, etc. corresponds with natural categories of male/female, animate/inanimate,

etc. Most **dialects** of modern English have natural gender, so nouns referring to female human beings and domestic animals (*girl*, *cow*) are associated with pronouns *she*, *her* etc., male humans and some animals (*boy*, *bull*) with *he/his* etc., and inanimate objects and non-domestic animals (*table*, *caterpillar*) with *it*, *its*.

non-standard   16

A **dialect** or a word, pronunciation or grammatical construction that is different from, but not inferior to, the standard or that used in the standard.

object   79

The part of a **clause** or sentence that refers to the person, thing, etc. that receives the action of the verb. In English the object normally appears after the verb, as in 'I shot the sheriff' where *sheriff* is the object.

parody   16

An imitation of a piece of writing that is closely modelled on another (usually well-known) piece, for humorous purposes.

passive vocabulary   53

The set of words that a speaker knows or recognises, but does not use.

person   25

The category of grammar that distinguishes the first person, the speaker(s) or writer(s) of the sentence (*I*, *we*) from the second-person addressee(s) (*you*) and the third person, someone or something referred to that is neither the speaker nor the addressee (*he*, *him*, *she*, *her*, *it*, *they*).

phoneme/phonemic 111

A phoneme is a unit of pronunciation that can distinguish one word from another. A pair of words that differ only with respect to a single phoneme is called a minimal pair. In RP and Southern **accents** of British English, *put* and *putt* form a minimal pair, because the former has /ʊ/ and the latter /ʌ/, so these two are distinct phonemes in these varieties.

phonetic 50

This refers to all the sounds of speech, whether they are **phonemes** or **allophones** in any particular language. A phonetic transcription will be more detailed than a **phonemic** one, including features such as 'clear' vs. 'dark' /l/ etc.

phrase 8

A structure that contains more than one word, but, unlike a **clause**, does not contain a subject and a verb. Examples of phrases are *tired and emotional, Monday afternoon, public transport.*

pronoun 68

A word that can be substituted for a noun. These include personal pronouns (*I, me, we, us, you, he, him, she, her, it, they*); possessive pronouns (*my, mine, our, ours, your, yours, his, hers, its, their, theirs*); reflexive pronouns (*myself, ourselves, yourself, yourselves, himself, herself, itself, themselves*); and relative pronouns (*who, whom, whose, which, that*).

pronoun exchange 79

The phenomenon in certain **dialects** where the form usually associated with the subject in Standard English appears in **object** position and/or vice-versa, as in *Her said to I.*

proper noun 69

A noun referring to the name of a person, domestic animal, place etc., e.g. *Monica, Buttercup, Leeds.* These cannot take a definite or indefinite article in English, so we do not see *a Monica, the Leeds* unless we are referring to a person who is obsessively tidy, like Monica in *Friends* (you're such a Monica!), or the Leeds Building Society. In such cases, the nouns are no longer proper nouns since they do not refer to a specific person or place.

Received Pronunciation 29

The prestigious **accent** of British English, used as a reference variety in dictionaries and for teaching British English as a second or foreign language.

recessive 8

This refers to a feature that is less common or widespread than it used to be and that shows signs of eventually disappearing. Typically, a recessive feature will be confined to isolated rural **dialects** and/or the speech of older people.

referent 92

The person, thing, etc. referred to by a word. The referent of the word *chair* is a particular piece of furniture.

regionalism 84

The use in **dialect** literature or literary dialect of a word or grammatical construction that is associated with a regional dialect.

relative marker 96

A word used to refer to something previously mentioned. In Standard English, these are *who*, *which*, *whom*, *whose* and *that*. As in 'I read the book *which/that* you recommended', 'She's the woman *who* won the lottery'.

relative pronoun 23

A relative pronoun is used to link **clauses** by referring back to a noun that has appeared before it. Instead of linking two clauses with 'and': 'I read a book and it was interesting', we can say 'The book that I read was interesting'.

rhotic 41

An **accent** of English in which /r/ is pronounced when it appears after a vowel and before a **consonant** or the end of a word, as in *cart*, *car*.

salient 30

A feature that is recognised as typical of a particular **accent** or **dialect**, or that distinguishes one from another.

saying 22

A set of words that is traditional and proverbial and is preserved and transmitted in the same form over a long period of time, such as 'red sky at night, shepherds' delight' or 'where there's muck, there's brass'.

schwa 43

The name given to the vowel most commonly used in unstressed syllables in English, and the symbol used for this in the International Phonetic Alphabet /ə/.

semi-phonetic spelling 22

The use of **non-standard** spellings to indicate regional or non-standard pronunciations.

Sense Relation Network 62

A tool devised for the collection of **dialect** words, and used in the *Survey of Regional English* (SuRE). SRNs link together key concepts in the form of spider diagrams, and are based on the idea of 'mental maps', in which concepts are grouped together in the way that they are linked in the mind.

slang 7

Items of non-standard vocabulary that are not restricted to a geographical region and are characteristically short-lived. Slang tends to be used by a closed group of people, often united by common interests, such as surfers, bikers, etc., or by generational groups such as teenagers.

speech community 30

A group of speakers who share a set of linguistic norms, or evaluations of language. These speakers may use different forms but will agree about which forms are prestigious, which are associated with lower-class speakers, etc.

Standard English 16

The **dialect** used in formal or official writing and speech, and that taught as a second or foreign language. This may differ from one country to another, so that Standard British (rather, English) English, is different from Standard Australian English, etc.

subject 78

The part of a sentence that refers to the person, thing, etc., that 'performs' the action of the verb. In English, the **subject** usually comes before the verb. In the sentence 'The dog chased the postman', 'the dog' is the subject.

subjective reaction tests 30

A type of experiment in which participants are asked to give judgements about perceived qualities of speakers whose voices are played to them. The experiment is designed to elicit stereotyped reactions to **accents** and typically asks for evaluations of friendliness, honesty, intelligence, etc.

sub-standard 67

This term is rarely used in linguistics, except to contrast with **non-standard**, since it refers to something which is deficient rather than simply 'different' from the standard variety.

superlative 71

A form of the **adjective** or **adverb** that compares the degree of a quality of more than two nouns or verbs, and refers to the one that has that quality to the highest degree, such as *fittest/most healthy; fastest/most speedily*.

terms of endearment 21

Words or **phrases** used to signal affection or intimacy. Examples are *love, mate, pet, sunshine*, etc.

variable 30

In sociolinguistics, a variable is a unit that, in a particular variety, is subject to variation. The variants are the different forms it may take. For example, in British English, (h) is a variable which has two variants, /h/ and zero, in /hous/ or /aus/ for *house*.

velar nasal 47

The **consonant** formed by raising the back of the tongue towards the back of the mouth, and letting the air pass through the nose. This occurs in words where <n> appears before <g> or <k> in the spelling, such as *think, sing*.

vocalised 49

Turned into a vowel or vowel-like sound. Historically, /l/ has been vocalised in *half, psalm*, and in present-day English, it is vocalised in regional **accents** of London and the South East of England in e.g. *Paul, fault*.

Related titles from Routledge

A Survey of English Dialects: the Dictionary and Grammar
Clive Upton

This study provides material gathered by the "Survey of English Dialects" in alphabetical form. It contains around 17,000 headwords and includes detailed phonetic transcriptions. A separate section provides a systematic analysis of the syntactic patterns of the various dialects. It is a valuable tool for dialectologists worldwide.

Hb: 0–415–02029–8

Available at all good bookshops
For ordering and further information please visit:
www.routledge.com